ARCHBISHOP
SARAH
MULLALLY

ARCHBISHOP SARAH MULLALLY

AND TEN URGENT CHALLENGES FOR THE CHURCH OF ENGLAND

INTELLIGENT ♦ INSPIRATIONAL ♦ INCLUSIVE
SPIRITUAL BOOKS

First published in 2026 by
Darton, Longman and Todd Ltd
Unit 1, The Exchange
6 Scarbrook Road
Croydon CR0 1UH
editorial@darton-longman-todd.co.uk

This product conforms to the requirements of the European Union's General Product Safety Regulations (GPSR).
EU Authorised Representative for GPSR:
Easy Access System Europe –
Mustamäe tee 50, 10621 Tallinn, Estonia
gpsr.requests@easproject.com

Biographical chapter © Tim Wyatt 2026

The Separation of Church and Hate © Mark Oakley 2026

Facing Truth with Honesty © Eileen Harrop and AMEN CIC 2026

A Place for All Bodies © Emily Richardson 2026

Sitting Outside, Encountering Christ © Charlie Baczyk-Bell 2026

When Rights are Rolled Back, 'Let Justice Roll Like a River'
© Christina Beardsley 2026

Falling Among Thieves © Andrew Graystone 2026

Challenge Inequality, Change Practice, Deepen Spirituality
© Jon Kuhrt 2026

Hopes and Opportunities for the World © Ruth Valerio 2026

The Thread that Binds Us © Amatu Christian-Iwuagwu 2026

In the Bleeding Silence © Chantal Noppen 2026

Afterword © Rowan Williams 2026

'East of Eden: Gateshead' (page 62) and prayer on page 165
© Jon Swales and used by kind permission.

The right of each writer to be identified as author of their chapter has been asserted in accordance with the Copyright, Designs and Patents Act 1988.

ISBN: 978-1-917362-20-7

No part of this book may be used or reproduced in any manner for the purpose of training artificial intelligence technologies or systems.

A catalogue record for this book is available from
the British Library.

Printed and bound in Great Britain by Bell and Bain, Glasgow

CONTENTS

	ABOUT THIS BOOK	7
	ARCHBISHOP SARAH MULLALLY: THE BIOGRAPHY Tim Wyatt	9
1	THE SEPARATION OF CHURCH AND HATE *Spirituality and the Church of England* Mark Oakley	43
2	FACING TRUTH WITH HONESTY *Nationalism, Racism and the Church of England* Eileen Harrop	57
3	A PLACE FOR ALL BODIES *Welcoming and Empowering Disabled People in the Church of England* Emily Richardson	77
4	SITTING OUTSIDE, ENCOUNTERING CHRIST: *The Church of England, LGBTQIA Inclusion and Same-Sex Marriage* Charlie Baczyk-Bell	91
5	WHEN RIGHTS ARE ROLLED BACK, 'LET JUSTICE ROLL LIKE A RIVER' *Trans and Non-Binary People and the Church of England* Christina Beardsley SMMS	105

6   FALLING AMONG THIEVES: 119
    UNDERSTANDING AND
    RESPONDING TO CHURCH-
    RELATED ABUSE
    Abuse, Safeguarding and the Church of England
    Andrew Graystone

7   CHALLENGE INEQUALITY, 135
    CHANGE PRACTICE, DEEPEN
    SPIRITUALITY
    Poverty and the Church of England
    Jon Kuhrt

8   HOPES AND OPPORTUNITIES 149
    FOR THE WORLD
    Climate Care and the Church of England
    Ruth Valerio

9   THE THREAD THAT BINDS US 169
    The Challenge of Global Anglican Unity
    Amatu Christian-Iwuagwu

10 IN THE BLEEDING SILENCE 191
    Mission and the Church of England
    Chantal Noppen

AFTERWORD 203
Rowan Williams, Former Archbishop of
Canterbury

About This Book

This book has been written and published to mark and to accompany the installation of Sarah Mullally as the 106th Archbishop of Canterbury. It serves as a helpful introduction to the life, ministry, experience and character of Archbishop Sarah, courtesy of a biography written by journalist Tim Wyatt, and further chapters authored by ten Anglican writers, each of whom has been asked to write about a particular challenge facing the new primate and the Church of England under her leadership. The book ends with an Afterword by Dr Rowan Williams, the 104th Archbishop of Canterbury.

Darton, Longman and Todd would like to thank all of the contributors for writing their chapters at such short notice, with care and enthusiasm, candour, clarity and hope.

The writers are:

Tim Wyatt is a freelance journalist who has written for *The Guardian, The Times, The Economist and The Daily Telegraph*, most often on religion and social affairs. He hosts a podcast, Matters of Life and Death, and writes a weekly email newsletter, The Critical Friend.

The Very Revd Dr Mark Oakley is Dean of Southwark, and Whitelands Professorial Fellow in Christianity and Contemporary Issues, Roehampton

University. He is the author of several books on literature and spirituality, including *The Splash of Words: Believing in Poetry* which won the international Michael Ramsey Prize for theological writing.

The Revd Canon Eileen Khean Geok Harrop is the elected Chair of AMEN (Anglican Minority Ethnic Network), the independent CIC described by the Church of England's Racial Justice Unit as 'the umbrella ethnocultural network', which is both critical friend and challenge to the Church. Of Chinese ethnicity, Eileen is a member of Teahouse, the network for ordinands and clergy of Chinese heritage. Eileen is the Incumbent Priest of 4 rural parishes and a church plant in Durham Diocese, and the Diocese UKME Advisor and Canon for Pilgrimage. Until 2025, she was one of the 3 elected UKME Participant Observers on the House of Bishops.

Emily Richardson is co-author of *At the Gates: Disability, Justice and the Churches* and is a trustee of Inclusive Church. She works in communications for a busy church in South West London and enjoys writing, reading, theatre trips, watching numerous boxsets and resting.

The Revd Dr Charlie Baczyk-Bell is a priest and a forensic psychiatrist. He is Associate Vicar of St John the Divine, Kennington, in the Diocese of Southwark, Visiting Scholar at Sarum College, and the Fellow in Medicine and Public Theology at Girton College, Cambridge.

The Revd Dr Christina (Tina) Beardsley SMMS is a Visiting Scholar at Sarum College, with Permission to Officiate in the Dioceses of London and Southwark. Tina has co-authored a trilogy of

About This Book

books about being transgender and Christian, two of them published by Darton, Longman and Todd.

Andrew Graystone is a writer and theologian who advocates for victims and survivors of church-related abuse. His doctoral thesis was on the theology of touch in digital culture. His book *Bleeding for Jesus: John Smyth and the Cult of Iwerne Camps* was published by Darton, Longman and Todd in 2025.

Jon Kuhrt is the CEO of Hope into Action. He has worked with people affected by homelessness for over 30 years and is a former government adviser on rough sleeping and was CEO of the West London Mission. He hosts the Grace+Truth blog and lives in Streatham, South London.

Dr Ruth Valerio is one of the leading voices in the UK Church on issues of climate, environment and global social justice. She pioneered the Eco Church movement and is Programmes and Advocacy Director at Embrace the Middle East. Canon Theologian at Rochester cathedral, Ruth is a sought-after writer and speaker.

The Revd Preb Dr Amatu Christian-Iwuagwu is an Anglican priest, Christian leader engaged in faith and culture, and diocesan leader in the Church of England. He served as Director of Mission and Racial Justice, and is a Church Commissioner and General Synod member, combining parish ministry with strategic leadership, teaching, and a commitment to justice, reconciliation, and mission.

The Revd Chantal Noppen is an AuDHD Anglican priest and National Coordinator of Inclusive Church. A practical theologian whose work explores the intersections of theology, justice and lived experience, with particular interest on overlooked people and places. She is passionate about how grace is practised, resisted and recognised in the ordinary, messy realities of everyday life.

Lord Rowan Williams of Oystermouth was Archbishop of Canterbury between 2002 and 2012. Prior to that he was Archbishop of Wales for three years, and Bishop of Monmouth for eleven years. He is acknowledged internationally as an outstanding theologian, writer and teacher, and has written a number of bestselling books of faith and thought.

Archbishop Sarah Mullally: The Biography

Tim Wyatt

Much was made, when Sarah Mullally was announced as the next Archbishop of Canterbury in October 2025, of her background. 'The nurse who became archbishop' was the social media post from the Health Secretary Wes Streeting. Observers marvelled at how the Church of England's incoming leader had previously risen to the peak of an entirely different career, becoming England's Chief Nursing Officer back in the 1990s while still in her thirties, before chucking it all in and starting again as a lowly vicar.

But behind the headlines, not much is known about Mullally's life and times. A reserved and private person, she has been relatively reticent about her life before she became a bishop. To try and piece together her story, I've spoken to dozens of people who have worked with her, both as a nurse, a bureaucrat, a priest, and finally as a bishop. I've also combed through media coverage going back 30 years, long before anyone knew this understated yet hyper-competent nurse would become the nation's first female archbishop. Mullally was also kind enough to give me an interview as well, which has helped in fleshing out some of the earlier stages of her life. The picture that emerges is both strikingly ordinary and yet also fascinating and unexpected in places.

Woking to London

Sarah Elisabeth Bowser was born on 26 March 1962 in Woking. The daughter of Michael, an electrical engineer, and Ann, a hairdresser turned stay-at-home mum, Sarah was one of four children in a happy and largely unremarkable family. Growing up in classic Surrey suburbia with two sisters and a brother, Sarah remembers a contented childhood filled with cycle trips across town, French horn lessons, and football games with her brother (until she was barred after accidentally injuring one of his friends in an over-zealous tackle).

Aged 11, she started at her local comprehensive, the Winston Churchill School. Here she thrived, particularly enjoying maths and sciences, although she was also diagnosed with dyslexia while doing her O levels. She already had an inkling of what her future might hold, feeling increasingly drawn towards healthcare. This sense of a call arose at the same time as she became a Christian, aged 16.

The family had long been somewhat tepid churchgoers, mostly continuing due to the commitment of Sarah's grandparents rather than parents Michael and Ann. But it was during a confirmation class that teenage Sarah was asked if she'd yet made a 'personal commitment' to Christ. 'I'm not sure I knew what that meant or if I had, so we prayed,' she later recalled.

After O levels, she moved a few miles across town to Woking College for sixth form. By this time, she was already asking herself what Jesus wanted her to do with her life and despite the urging of friends to consider the Church she dismissed it, in part because at the time women could not be ordained. After narrowing her options to medicine or nursing, she decided on the latter, seeing it as a more 'holistic' effort to care for people. This prompted her choice of A levels: maths, chemistry and zoology. 'There was no doubt in sixth form, my nursing was a vocation,' she has said. 'It was a sense of call.'

When she finished school in 1980, Sarah Bowser followed this call out of Woking and moved to London, a city which had often felt impossibly distant despite its proximity to her suburban Surrey childhood. She enrolled as a student nurse at St Thomas's Hospital, nestled up against the Thames in central London. Unusually, however, she decided to become a degree nurse.

At that time only one in twelve nurses chose the university route, but Sarah was convinced it was necessary to become the kind of nurse she felt she was going to be. 'Nursing at its best is the art of the application of the science,' she reflected decades later, and the university path which combined classwork with on-the-ward placements offered a 'theoretical framework' to embed her practice. But her desire for book learning did not diminish the centrality of person-to-person care. 'If you don't have a fundamental belief in humanity, all of that goes by the by,' she told the *Church Times* in an interview almost 30 years later. 'If someone is struggling to drink a cup of tea, you help them to drink it. At the end of the day, we're there to care.'

For four years Sarah juggled her studies between what was then South Bank Polytechnic with her apprenticeship at the Florence Nightingale School of Nursing at St Thomas's, a short walk away. Nightingale had founded the world's first modern nursing school 120 years earlier believing technical training, undergirded by statistics and research, was paramount. And yet the Lady with the Lamp was also hailed as an angelic bedside presence. Sarah Bowser later said she too sought to combine academic and scientific rigour with humane and compassionate care in her own nursing.

Years later, when Chief Nursing Officer, she wrote in *Nursing Standard* magazine in praise of one of her nursing heroes, a woman called Denise Whitehouse she'd met at St Thomas's. In her tribute, we see the threads of what the now Sarah Mullally believed made up outstanding nursing. Whitehouse too blended clinical excellence with a humane presence, Mullally wrote: 'She was a tremendous communicator and clinical role model. She walked the talk.' She set high technical standards while offering a kind and attentive presence to the patients on her gastrointestinal ward as they faced life-changing surgeries.

It was while she was still training that she first met Eamonn Mullally, first crossing paths when he visited his brother living in the same Stockwell halls of residence. Before long, Eamonn had joined Sarah and a group of other twenty-somethings at a nearby church, St Stephen's, which they had stumbled into by chance one Sunday.

Long before they married, the pair became a fixture in the conservative evangelical congregation. So much so that the vicar, Christopher Guinness, roped Sarah in to help look after his older children while his youngest son Jack was being born during one of her summers. Guinness's wife later recalled how the trainee nurse was a 'very reliable, safe pair of hands' for anything that needed doing in the parish. 'Sarah was steady and grounded and willing to get stuck in,' Guinness wrote years later in *The Times*.

Her time at St Stephen's, in and out of the bustling vicarage and part of a thriving group of young professionals, was a happy if busy one. The church sat in a diverse and very much un-gentrified slice of South London, at a time when communal tensions during the Thatcher years were running high. Just a few years earlier and a mile further south, the Brixton riots had erupted. Many in the multicultural congregation at St Stephen's had their own stories to tell of prejudice and outright racism, including from the police.

Rising up the ranks

Sarah Bowser spent two years as a staff nurse at St Thomas's – mostly on a gastrointestinal ward – and thrived within a team of easy-going nurses and doctors. 'It was great fun,' she remembered. 'There were difficult moments, patients got ill, but we had some good laughs.' In 1986 she moved just over the Thames to Chelsea to work at the Royal Marsden Hospital, the world's first specialist cancer hospital. Here she began to specialise in oncology, enjoying the opportunities at the generously-resourced hospital. She also married Eamonn in 1987 in a ceremony held at St Stephen's. A year later, just four years into her career, the now Sarah Mullally was promoted to ward sister a short distance across West London at the Westminster Hospital in Fulham. She now managed a team of nurses and showed such aptitude for this responsibility she was swiftly promoted again just two years later, aged 30, to become the senior nurse for her West London health authority.

It was a time of huge change and flux. Her authority was running a brand-new hospital amid a raft of wider NHS reorganisations. But it was also a time of opportunity for bright, ambitious nurses. One younger nurse who worked under her recalls Mullally being both 'very kind and pragmatic', as well as a role model for a new breed of degree-educated nurse. As chief nurse Mullally was expected to set a culture for the authority's nurses and write policies, but she did not stay cooped up in her office. She regularly walked the wards, never forgetting junior nurses' names to say hello. One nurse recalls a reserved character, 'very quiet but very kind, very thoughtful and an amazing communicator'. Her faith was not front and centre yet it seemed to seep through in how she behaved, the nurse said.

Mullally was also heavily in favour of further education, ensuring her nurses were offered study leave on the same terms as the doctors, an unusual policy of parity for the era. She followed her own advice too, studying for a Master's degree in interprofessional health and welfare, once again from South Bank University, alongside her senior nurse position. As her career moved away from the wards she wanted to buttress her knowledge with more theory and strategy.

At the same time as her career accelerated, life at home was also becoming busier. In 1991 Sarah and Eamonn welcomed their first child, Grace. In a sign of her unquenchable work ethic, she decided to use her 'free' time while on maternity leave to complete her Master's dissertation. The family were still settled at St Stephen's, and it was here (after the C of E had finally come round to women's ordination), that she returned – prompted by the urging of friends – to those stirrings from sixth form. Might God still want her to enter ministry after all? This train of thought was complicated for a time by the trenchant opposition to female priests by her vicar of the time; his lack of a direct referral made it difficult to find out how the discernment process with the local Diocese of Southwark worked.

Throughout the rest of the 1990s, Mullally glided ever upwards, becoming by 1994 the director of nursing and deputy chief executive of the Chelsea and

Westminster Hospital. Still only in her early 30s, she was probably the youngest director of nursing in the entire NHS. One further step removed from the wards, Mullally's job now involved examining the latest research to see how to improve practice, developing new initiatives, and increasingly the growing area known as patient experience.

The NHS was in turmoil too, as the government implemented a divide between the purchasers of healthcare services and the providers of them. Now, even in the publicly-funded health service, hospitals and authorities had to compete with each other to secure multi-million pound contracts. In the crowded field of London hospitals, this bunfight for resources in the 1990s could become intense.

Despite the backbiting, endless reorganisations and rounds of redundancies a chief nurse at a neighbouring health authority remembered Mullally always kept her cool and remained pleasant: 'She was a very nice person, but I don't say that she particularly stood out.'

Amidst this challenging and demanding role, her son Liam was born in 1995. The workaholic Mullally wasn't content with simply juggling motherhood and NHS management. Having navigated the traditionalism of her own vicar (the minister would not even be present in the building when she preached) she began training in 1998 at the South East Institute for Theological Education (SEITE), just four years after women priests were first ordained.

SEITE itself was also a pioneering institution, the Church's first ever non-residential training scheme for clergy. Although Mullally was convinced she would quit her hospital job for a full-time post once ordained, SEITE's part-time course mostly fitted in well around her hectic work life (although she must be the only ordinand in Church history to cry off their final residential training weekend after being called into an urgent meeting with the Prime Minister).

Those plans to commit to the vicar's life were jettisoned just a year into her training when, in 1999, she was promoted yet again. In a bid to demonstrate a new broom, the New Labour health secretary Frank Dobson decided to make a point of hiring his next Chief Nursing Officer for England (CNO) – normally a senior civil servant in the autumn of their career – straight out of the hospitals: Sarah Mullally.

Aged just 37, she was the youngest CNO in history. In a speech a few months into the post, she laid out her vision for nursing – unchanged since those early days at South Bank Polytechnic almost two decades earlier. Compassionate care hand-in-hand with technical excellence. 'Patients want nurses to be knowledgeable and technically proficient, but they also want them to care,' she said. 'I don't believe that caring and academic ability are incompatible.'

In the heart of Whitehall

Sarah Mullally's time at the Department for Health was dominated by major reforms to nursing, as the profession continued to modernise within a fast-changing NHS. It was a boom time for the health service, as New Labour lavished it with funds from a thriving economy. A target of hiring 60,000 new nurses was set and met. Although she initially batted away calls to bring back the traditional matron, just a few years later she was championing what she called the 'modern matron': 'a golden opportunity for sisters to reclaim the wards'.

Encouraging nurses to pursue more training and professional development was a major theme too, and Mullally unlocked several pots of cash for further study. She also pushed forward expansions to prescribing powers for nurses and steered through the shift to make all nurses train via university-taught degrees. Alongside the emphasis on professional development and boosting nurses' technical skills was a renewed focus on patient care. Mullally personally spearheaded the launch of Essence of Care in 2001, a national strategy to improve and standardise how nurses looked after patients. By 2003 she was taking a victory lap in the industry magazine *Nursing Standard*: 'We now have more nurses who are better organised, better educated, better equipped, more responsive, better led and more autonomous.'

As she plugged away in Whitehall, her vicar training at SEITE came to an end with ordination in 2001. She could not continue serving at conservative St Stephen's now she was a priest, so a new church was found. Monday to Friday would be spent at the Department for Health working on nursing strategy and development, while on Sundays she was an unpaid curate in the benefice of Battersea Fields in South London. This was a recent amalgamation of three churches, two moderate evangelical parishes with a third more liberal Anglo-Catholic in flavour.

Mullally spent most of her time ministering to the multicultural housing estate congregations of the more familiarly evangelical St Saviour's and St George's. The vicar, Geoff Vevers, secured his high-profile curate thanks to a family connection through his wife and Mullally's sister, later saying he 'jumped at the chance to have someone so gifted on our team'.

Despite her pressurised role as CNO, the workhorse Mullally got typically stuck in at Battersea. On Sundays she would preach and lead worship, and would even chisel out time most weeks to lead evening Bible studies. Vevers and others marvelled at her ability to multi-task and her uncomplaining 'hard-working ethos'. 'She was just so competent in everything she did and seemed to know by instinct what was involved in church leadership and pastoral care,' the vicar said. And not just a proficient automaton, but a personable presence in the parish too. Vevers recalled Mullally coming in on a rare day off and literally rolling up her sleeves to help clean the church's kitchen without complaint. 'She wasn't shy of getting her hands dirty. Everyone took to her and appreciated her. She was able to relate to all manner of people with a warm and caring manner.'

Occasionally she was sent to the more liberal corner of the benefice, All Saints, to gain experience. The priest there, Alan Gadd, remembered her being open-minded and comfortable with his congregants despite being clearly out of her comfort zone. During her visits she developed a pastoral relationship with some people at All Saints, including one couple wrestling with a diagnosis of Parkinson's. When this parishioner finally succumbed to the disease years later, Mullally – by now Bishop of London – replied promptly and kindly to an email letting her know, having instantly remembered the family she'd not seen for over a decade. 'She was quite impressive really,' Gadd concluded.

Starting again

In 2004, Mullally made what seemed a startling decision. After five years as the leading nurse in England, she decided to abandon her burgeoning Whitehall career and instead double down on the Church. She announced she would be resigning as CNO to become a full-time curate at Battersea Fields.

The prevailing tenor of the media coverage at the time was mild incredulity, mixed with endless references to how Mullally, aged only 42, was exchanging her £115,000 a year Department for Health salary (more than £200,000 in today's money) to earn a paltry £17,500 as a lowly priest. Mullally later said the decision to give up the CNO job was the 'hardest' she ever made. She likened leaving behind her secure civil service job as a leap of faith: 'There is this moment where you feel as though you were drowning ... what on earth have I done ... before you pop up and think "Actually I'm pretty glad I did that".'

Mullally has since said she is most proud of the culture change she introduced into the NHS, replacing 'NHS knows best' with a patient-centred ethos. She was universally hailed as an effective moderniser of nursing in tributes paid when she stood down. But alongside all the important reforms around degree-level training, professional development, modern matrons and nurse prescribing, it was 'old-fashioned nursing care that mattered to her most', one director of nursing told the *Nursing Standard*. 'Her drive to reinvent the "essence of care" in nursing and involve patients in decisions will be her most important legacy.'

She was also praised for her consistent championing of ethnic minority nurses into positions of leadership, and determination to tackle racism and discrimination. In her valedictory interview, Mullally herself recommended her successor not be another white woman, or even worse, a man (as had just happened for the Scottish CNO). Although women dominated the profession, male nurses seemed to rise through the ranks much more easily, the normally conciliatory Mullally observed somewhat caustically.

Having laid down her nursing career, Mullally spent two more years completing her curacy at Battersea Fields. For all the family's income had taken a colossal hit, her children – now both at school – hugely enjoyed having a mother free to do morning drop-offs rather than tied up in endless meetings. To crown her now ended first career, she was made Dame Commander of the Order of the British Empire in 2005 for services to nursing. A year later she completed her second Master's degree, this time in pastoral theology from Heythrop College.

As she came to the end of her curacy the Bishop of Croydon Nick Baines was in the middle of reorganising ministry in the South London suburb of Sutton, where three parish priests had all moved on at the same time. One bishop in the diocese felt their rising star in Battersea should be carefully shepherded on to a junior associate vicar role, arguing the former chief nurse did not yet have enough church experience to lead a parish solo. But Baines would have none of it. Knowing she was more than capable, he encouraged her to apply for the new role of Team Rector for Sutton in 2006, the three churches now lumped together into one benefice.

It was another trailblazing role. As the first ever Team Rector in Sutton, Mullally had to build a team from scratch while trying to meld together three disparate congregations. In the end, she and one other full-time paid priest were licensed to all three churches, sharing the load across the benefice in what was then an unusual arrangement for the C of E. 'Clergy need other clergy,' she later said. 'It's much better to work as a team.'

She did not stand out for overseeing stratospheric growth or dazzling missional initiatives, but was, as always, quietly competent and reliable. 'She got a grip on things, brought order to it,' Baines said. 'I was confident about it and about her.'

The team in Sutton had been somewhat dispirited when she arrived, as a handful of part-time unpaid clergy tried to hold things together knocking about in cold, damp barn-like Victorian buildings. While some traditionalist elements in the congregations remained uncomfortable with the still novel presence of a woman in a dog collar, another of the clergy who helped out in Sutton recalled Mullally bringing a sense of 'refreshment' to the newly-formed benefice.

Alongside her parish ministry, Mullally continued to build up other clergy, including one minister in the team who was also a detective inspector in the Metropolitan Police. She began training curates too, one of whom remembers a 'very happy' time learning under her in Sutton. Grace and Liam were both well into their school years, but without the full-time nanny she had employed while CNO, Mullally found her days full balancing work and family needs. Jane Cresswell, one of Mullally's curates, praised her then boss for modelling a healthy path through 'family life and my responsibilities'. It was no surprise given her experience in unleashing nurses' untapped skills that Cresswell found in Mullally someone who ably combined hands-on guidance with a 'generous encouragement to develop my own gifts in ministry'.

Mullally also continued to work with the Diocese of Southwark in training clergy in leadership. In a *Church Times* interview from this period she reflected on her time at the pinnacle of nursing and now leading in another institution: 'We often confuse leadership with status, power, and money – not enabling and facilitating.' Having been once at the heart of the Whitehall machine, she now relished being on the outside. 'Big organisations are slow, thick-skinned, strong, powerful. Fleas are frisky, agile, vulnerable, and irritating. I see myself more as a flea now.'

Breaking the stained-glass ceiling
In that same interview, she insisted she had no grand career plan to match her rise through nursing in the Church. Instead, she felt content where she was. And

yet, after five or so years leading ministry in Sutton, higher-ups in the Church began to circle around her. It was 2011, and moves in the Church's parliament, the General Synod, to finally allow women to become bishops not just priests were gathering steam.

June Osborne, then Dean of Salisbury Cathedral and one of the most senior women knocking their heads against the Church's stained-glass ceiling, had grown frustrated with progress at getting women promoted. Concerned the pipeline was blocking up as her too modest peers failed to push for jobs their breezily confident male counterparts landed, Osborne launched a development programme for talented women priests called Leading Women.

Mullally applied for the second cohort of Leading Women, and spent a year being encouraged to lift her sights beyond humble parish ministry to bigger and broader roles. She made such an impression Osborne invited her back to help run the following year of the programme.

Her bishop back in South London, Baines, had designs on making her one of his archdeacons, but Osborne nicked in there first. A vacancy as Canon Treasurer at Salisbury Cathedral came up in 2012, and with some gentle nudging Mullally applied and won the role. An only slightly rueful Baines reflected how despite her total lack of vanity or ambition, it had always been obvious to him his Team Rector of Sutton was destined for greater things. 'Sarah never comes across as someone who is ambitious,' he said. 'She's not an ego-merchant. She comes across as someone who's measured, accomplished, and she's clearly weighed up what she's taking on so she doesn't go into it blind.'

For Mullally, having come out of conservative evangelicalism and led middle of the road to slightly Anglo-Catholic worship in Sutton, the cathedral was a chance to broaden her horizons and develop her 'liturgical confidence'. 'If you can preside in a cathedral, you can preside anywhere'.

Despite the name, the role of Canon Treasurer had little to do with finance. Instead, Mullally's new job focused on the buildings and assets of Salisbury Cathedral, the thirteenth-century masterpiece she now called home. Among the 'treasures' she was now responsible for was the cathedral's ultra-rare copy of one of the four original Magna Cartas, as well as a clock said to be the oldest working timepiece on earth. She was also the senior cleric responsible for the cathedral's long-running renovation programme, begun some thirty years earlier and still with a decade left to completion.

Mullally plunged herself into committee meetings, drawing together teams and handling administration and bureaucracy with her typical competence and lack of fuss. Nick Holtam, the Bishop of Salisbury at the time, who was a close neighbour of Mullally living in the Cathedral Close, said the one-time chief nurse clearly knew how to run a meeting efficiently, but with a deft touch which allowed others to feel they had been heard. Mullally's prodigious work ethic shone through once more; no time was wasted and things just got sorted.

One diocesan staffer from that time remembers how his colleagues would 'rave' about Mullally's skill in committees and 'bringing business to fruition'. Osborne agreed, describing her former colleague as an incredibly effective operator. Unlike most clergy, 'she knows operationally how to get something done,' the dean mused. 'That may not sound the most romantic or heroic, but actually it's hugely helpful to have.'

But alongside her Stakhanovite work rate was a pastoral heart, observers remembered. Osborne often sent out her Canon Treasurer as the cathedral spokesperson during tricky public meetings or to sell plans to sceptical stakeholders. Mullally's measured and calm presence soothed agitated locals and smoothed over problems before they arose. 'People trust her; they instantly see somebody who is compassionate and humane, kind, generous,' Osborne observed. 'She's an extraordinarily good manager of people.' Mullally would often refer back to her nursing background, even in the rarefied settings of the medieval cathedral. Holtam said she was instinctively pastoral and cared for others, which quickly earned their trust.

And not all of this was for her institution's strategic benefit. Not long after Mullally arrived, another cathedral canon, the precentor Tom Clammer, was diagnosed with multiple sclerosis. The news came as a shock to Clammer, then in his mid-30s, but his former nurse colleague quickly sprang into action.

More than a decade later, Clammer remembered with fondness how Mullally offered support and advice as he and his wife navigated the early years of his diagnosis. 'Sarah is an absolutely wonderful person to whom I owe a very great deal,' he said. He remembered how she brought 'compassion and priestly care' as she ministered not just to him amid health crisis but the wider cathedral community. And once again the combination of technical competence with pastoral care shone through, Clammer added: 'That capacity to be both an efficient senior cleric but not to lose the absolute centre of her pastoral calling was a hallmark of her ministry in Salisbury.' Despite her moving on from Salisbury to bigger and bigger roles, Mullally has stayed in touch with Clammer, who considers her a friend to this day.

If her administrative nous and pastoral skills were not in question, Mullally's liturgical sensibilities were less secure when she arrived in Salisbury. Osborne said it was clear to her from day one that Mullally was destined for episcopal ministry (even if the synod had not yet quite managed to find a way to pass the necessary legislation). But to prepare her for that she had to 'find her voice' in a larger setting.

Mullally joined the team of three canons and Osborne who together managed a rota of morning prayer each day, along with four or five services on Sundays. 'She's not the strongest preacher in the world,' her former boss remarked, but she used the time in Salisbury to work on this less comfortable part of ministry.

Others also noticed her woodenness in the pulpit, including Holtam who said Mullally was well aware public speaking was not her strongest suit. One former member of the cathedral congregation vividly recalled hearing her first sermon, and not because of its rhetorical power. 'She was a very nice person, instantly quite warm, but not much personal presence at the altar,' he remembered. But over time she learned to relax and inhabit her role leading worship and prayer for congregations in their hundreds, if not thousands. In the end, what was needed from her was not soaring oratory but 'integrity and consistency, benevolence and competence', the former bishop Holtam insisted.

Down to Devon

As her horizons rapidly expanded in Salisbury, attention naturally began to turn to what could be next. In 2014 the synod approved the women bishops legislation and the next year Libby Lane smashed the stained-glass ceiling when she acceded to the see of Stockport as the Church's first-ever female bishop. Already, Mullally had told Holtam she felt she'd mastered the technical side of her expanded role in the cathedral. 'And that was the point at which we began to talk about the possibility of episcopacy,' he said.

Mullally herself has insisted she never had grand

designs on promotion. She was leading evensong late in 2012 while the first women bishops bill heartbreakingly failed by just a handful of votes at the synod. It was only when several people after the service assumed she was primarily disappointed because this would frustrate her personal ambitions that it dawned on her she was widely seen as a future bishop.

As one of the 'most competent people I've ever met', Holtam had no doubts about her capacity to take on the role. But he still thought she had more to learn about the 'spiritualities of the job, rather than the mechanics of the job'. And so when he recommended she be added to the secret list of potential bishops held at Lambeth Palace, it was as a future suffragan bishop rather than a diocesan. In that more junior role she could move more gradually through the ranks, learning the ropes as pastor to the pastors without the added burden of leading the diocese. Of course she wouldn't remain a suffragan very long, 'but I thought it might be an important step for her,' Holtam said.

Despite her rapid ascent, her colleagues insist there was no 'hint of ambition' within the former CNO. Her three years in Salisbury felt longer to many in the Cathedral Close, given how embedded Mullally became. Rather than nakedly using the Canon Treasurer job as a stepping stone to bigger things, the former dean Osborne recalls a total lack of self-promotion. 'She behaved as if this was her entire vocation. There's a very settled spirit in Sarah,' Osborne said. 'But then, I'm a realist and I knew the day we appointed her she wouldn't be in Salisbury forever. The job had been done. She had learned how to inhabit the space.' Regardless, Mullally had to be persuaded by Holtam to take seriously the offer to become the Bishop of Crediton, when that offer arrived in 2015.

In this brave new world, the longlist of names

sent by Lambeth Palace to the new-ish Bishop of Exeter Robert Atwell to fill his vacant Crediton post was decidedly cross-gender. Among them, thanks to Holtam, was the Canon Treasurer of Salisbury Cathedral.

Atwell can no longer recall what exactly drew his appointing committee to shortlist Mullally (she was in the end the only women of four candidates), but he well remembers the quality of her interview. It was both the shortest – 'Sarah answers the question, and when she's answered it, she stops' – but also by far the best. She was the unanimous choice of the committee to be Bishop of Crediton.

Mullally's patch within the diocese included the city of Exeter itself as well as the more remote northern parts of Devon. As she settled into her new episcopal digs (a three-bedroom Edwardian semi in the town of Tiverton), Mullally volunteered to also take on the thorny areas of safeguarding and finance, on top of her suffragan responsibilities. In between long trips in the car to visit her scattered parishes, she joined diocesan committee meetings and tried to inject greater rigour and professionalism.

Atwell repeatedly described her as a 'team player' rather than a lone ranger seeking to boost her own position, as well as 'pro to her fingertips' who valued 'good process'. A decade after she had moved on from her civil service apogee, Mullally was back once more leading large teams of people and trying to drive through change. Although unafraid of conflict, Mullally sought to cajole and persuade rather than bulldoze her way through her new diocese. Nick McKinnel, the diocese's other suffragan bishop in Plymouth, recalls her focus on strategy and process helped balance out his and Atwell's more freewheeling relaxed approach.

She looked after Devon's hospital chaplains, chaired the Mid Devon show, and generally threw herself into the life of a rural suffragan bishop. Because of its remoteness from the population centres on the south coast, North Devon's churches had a spirit of independence, but Mullally worked hard – assiduously visiting and encouraging when she could – to knit them into the rest of the diocese.

Even as she settled into her new life in rural Devon, she was regularly hopping aboard early morning trains at Tiverton Parkway for the three-and-half-hour journey back up to London. Within months of her arrival as a bishop, London and the national Church began their inexorable pull. In 2016 she became an independent governor of King's College London, and the same year was asked to take the lead on a troubling safeguarding case. Her first foray into national Church politics saw her tasked with implementing recommendations from a damning review into a poorly handled case of historic attempted rape by a prominent 1970s priest. The survivor in question had requested one of the Church's new crop of women bishops get the job, a more trustworthy option than the same old discredited male bishops.

It was not a happy breakthrough for Mullally, however. The recommendations got bogged down in recrimination and hostility, and years later the survivor would say Mullally had been well-meaning but quickly 'hoovered up' by the impenetrable institution. 'She didn't want to grasp the wider issues,' he said in 2019. 'I eventually got very frustrated.'

This setback did not harm Mullally's standing with the hierarchy in London. The following year the Living in Love and Faith (LLF) initiative began, an ambitious consultation and research project to map out the Church's thinking on sexuality in response to calls from the synod for better inclusion for gay people. Mullally was tasked with leading the

LLF sub-committee poring into what the social and biological sciences had to say.

Back in Devon, there were other challenges for only the fourth woman ever to be consecrated a bishop in the C of E. The Diocese of Exeter had a small but thriving minority of parishes which were unreconciled to women's ordination. Both of Atwell and McKinnel's predecessors refused to ordain women and Mullally was breaking ground simply by being in the room.

Atwell had been determined to correct the balance with a pro-women bishop and yet knew he was throwing Mullally into the lion's den. 'Sarah did encounter hostility and that must have cost her dearly,' he reflected. 'I know it did. She's always boldly going where no woman has gone before.' For the first time, Mullally was grappling with overseeing other clergy who rejected her calling and her authority.

Rather than stand on her rights or provoke confrontation, she typically approached with graciousness and sensitivity. McKinnel saw in this strains of her civil service background: 'Being fair to all and working through procedures properly and so on.' In truth, the role of Bishop of Crediton (which McKinnel himself had previously held) was a consensual job, not one rooted in authority. 'It's soft power, if it's power at all,' he said. 'It's encouraging and helping people along.' At this Mullally excelled, happy to talk to and work with anyone, including the conservatives who could not accept her ministry.

Having steeled himself for a backlash to his new female colleague, Atwell found himself impressed by how the former nurse carried herself, often gravitating towards those on the edges of rooms or meetings. 'Sarah the pastor, the healer,' he said. 'That's the side which shouldn't be lost when we talk about the institutional leader and strategic thinker.'

Back to London

It therefore came as something of a blow to Atwell when just two years into her tenure his Bishop of Crediton was 'pinched' by the Diocese of London to become their new bishop. Beyond the irritation was also astonishment at the promotion. It was a diocese with perhaps the country's strongest contingent of traditionalists opposed to women's ordination. He even questioned if it was worth his junior going through the intrusive interview process given she was certain never to get the gig.

Mullally herself was of a similar mind, assuming it was a hiding to nothing. 'They're not going to appoint a woman, and also not this woman,' she remembered thinking. 'You know, polytechnic girl, comprehensive school, dyslexia, non-residential training ...' 'I just found it inconceivable knowing London diocese that they would appoint a woman,' Atwell recalled. 'It was laughable, it would never happen. But God is full of surprises.' One member of the Crown Nominations Commission (CNC) convened to fill the vacant see said the committee went into deliberations on the basis London 'could never have a woman bishop because [of its] very big Anglo-Catholic and conservative enclave'. But as the interviews began, Mullally began to rise to the top. Her calm, measured approach won over the committee, who chose her in part as a 'safe pair of hands', the CNC member recalled.

The Diocese of London was a completely different kettle of fish to her role in Devon. Her predecessor Richard Chartres had ruled over the diocese for over 20 years. He was a patrician throwback to an older era of authoritarian prince-bishops, and also would not ordain women.

The five sub-areas of the diocese were larger by population and churchgoers than many entire dioceses elsewhere. And the area reserved for the

Bishop of London herself – the Two Cities of London and Westminster – was perhaps the most eccentric and daunting. A host of ancient parishes, revelling in their baffling rituals and traditions, many led by anti-women traditionalists bristling under the rule of their first ever female bishop.

There was certainly a 'fluttering in the dovecotes' among the more traditionalist churches (according to one bishop) when the news came down of Mullally's appointment, but in truth the former chief nurse found a system which worked. She largely stuck with the London Plan, the Chartres-era system of decentralisation which gives area bishops huge latitude and independence. Mullally went out of her way to build good relationships with Jonathan Baker, the Bishop of Fulham who catered for Anglo-Catholic traditionalists, and reassured his clergy she was not about to muscle in over their deeply-held convictions. 'She was very gracious in the way she would go along to traditional Anglo-Catholic ordinations and sit in the back and be happy not to be involved,' the area bishop said. 'She made it work.'

One senior female cleric familiar with the Two Cities area had also been flabbergasted that the CNC had chosen a woman as their new bishop. But she now admired how Mullally had found a middle ground of respecting traditionalists' positions while refusing to be cowed. 'She's very courageous about going into places where she knows that people do not accept that women ought to be priests at all, let alone ought to be the Bishop of London' the priest said. 'She just shows up and meets people as they are.'

Her gracious restraint when it came to respecting conservative traditions should not be mistaken for passivity, however. When she arrived in London the five area bishops were all white men. In her seven years at the helm, she has appointed four new bishops, and none are white men. Joanne Grenfell, appointed by Mullally as Bishop of Stepney in 2019, said she had assumed she wouldn't be deemed 'London' enough to get the role, but it became clear during the interviews that her putative boss wanted something 'fresh'.

The contrasts with her predecessor Chartres stretch way beyond simply gender and churchmanship. One of her area bishops described Chartres as a 'benevolent monarch' figure, who dispensed patronage at arms-length while hoarding authority. Mullally, in contrast, was a more available and collegial leader, and as always, was consistently praised for her pastoral ministry (and the fact that she was prompt in personally replying to emails).

'[Chartres] luxuriated in his undoubtedly impressive intellect and floated several feet above contradiction – we wouldn't have dared question him,' a senior diocesan official added. 'She is intelligent, highly competent, a lifelong learner, collaborates, admits and learns from her mistakes.' She swiftly ditched Chartres' chauffeur-driven official car, and tried to cycle to most of her appointments. Within the constraints of the London Plan she tried to stitch the five areas together more, visiting each area regularly and hosting away days with all her bishops and senior staff. One of the few things she kept a tight leash on, however, was safeguarding, with Grenfell reporting Mullally was 'uncompromising in insisting that safeguarding had to be a priority' and that she as diocesan was constantly kept in the loop.

And yet despite this more consensual dynamic, the new Bishop of London remained something of an enigma. Some felt they never really got to know the true Sarah behind the mask. She was still measured, thoughtful, always polite but perhaps a little distant, as she tried to hold together a fissiparous diocese. 'You could have an entire conversation or meeting without knowing precisely what she thinks personally about the particular issue, because she's very measured in the way that she draws in all of those different views,' observed the diocesan official.

'Sarah is personally warm and caring, but primarily a serious colleague, deeply professional and utterly committed,' was Grenfell's summation.

A degree of guardedness proved to be essential as Mullally got to grips with her fractious diocese. Her own Two Cities area included parishes from all ends of the spectrum, from the leading liberal powerhouse that is St Martin-in-the-Fields to the deeply conservative evangelical megachurch St Helen's Bishopsgate, whose spiky rector was regularly provoking conflict. Mixed in among them were numerous traditionalist Anglo-Catholic holdouts, suspicious of this comprehensive-educated former nurse with her sensible haircut and civil service jargon. Some even snidely took to calling her 'nursey' or 'bedpan' behind her back. Grenfell said she had also seen a 'streak of misogyny' from some of her clergy, especially from those trying to 'bully' Mullally out of her determination to introduce more accountability around safeguarding.

For all she was jarringly different from her predecessor Chartres, one of her bishops lamented her consensual conflict-avoidant style had limited meaningful change in the diocese. That said, he sympathised at her predicament of trying to keep a lid on the 'den of vipers' that were the vicars of the Two Cities: 'awkward clergy who have a habit of treating any authority badly'.

And it was in that Two Cities area where Mullally's biggest crisis arose. It had not taken the new bishop long after landing in the diocese to force out a man called Martin Sargeant, the head of operations for the Two Cities. Sargeant had connived his way to becoming Chartres' wheeler-dealer fixer, with vague if sweeping powers, and was indispensable for finding pots of cash for City churches' endless repairs. What was not yet known is that he was also dipping his hand into the till, ultimately stealing £5 million from the diocese over the years, for which he was later jailed for five years. As the arch-bureaucrat outsider Mullally began to drain the diocesan swamp, it swiftly became clear there was no room for murky figures like Sargeant.

Seeing the way the wind was blowing, the fixer resigned his post, but on his way out the door he handed on a list of innuendo, gossip and smears about his own clergy. This 'brain dump' was absorbed by the newly professionalised and beefed-up safeguarding team as a formal disclosure. There were 42 clergy on the list, but a bungled safeguarding investigation into one had tragic consequences in particular. Despairing at this Kafkaesque inquiry into Sargeant's evidence-free false allegations of sexual abuse, a vulnerable retired vicar called Alan Griffin took his own life in 2020.

Most of those who have worked with Mullally in London insist Sargeant was a toxic problem she inherited from Chartres. 'She didn't cause Martin Sargeant,' the senior official said. 'She dealt with him pretty early on in her watch.' But others worry her rigid insistence on proper (if not ruthless) safeguarding procedure without any filtering of Sargeant's lies first was partly to blame.

Under her the diocese has undoubtedly undergone a sea change in safeguarding standards, but not always for good, critics say. There are still clergy smarting not just from the clumsy handling of the other 41 names on the list, but also a separate episode a year or two later when Mullally launched a group disciplinary action against dozens of her own clergy for the technicality of not having their parish safeguarding details prominent enough on their websites.

Making her mark

As she strove to hold things together in her diocese, Mullally was also becoming a more central player in the national Church too. When the first wave of the COVID pandemic forced the closure of all C of E churches, Mullally was appointed chair of the committee steering the gradual re-opening and resumption of worship (thanks to her healthcare background).

Around the same time she also became the lead bishop for LLF. As research gave way to policy in 2022, she was at the forefront of decisions by the bishops to offer gay couples services of blessing in church for the first time. It was Mullally's job to sell this compromise solution (the Church's doctrine that marriage was only for straight couples would remain unchanged) to a deeply divided synod in 2023.

This was a challenge; she was passionate about offering better pastoral care to LGBT Christians (one of her personal priorities as Bishop of London was 'looking for the image of Christ in everyone'), and yet her pastoral instincts had to be tempered by championing a very Anglican fudge.

This blew up in her face as liberals felt betrayed while conservatives were outraged by the reforms. Ever the consensual figure and lacking any particular faction to speak up for her, Mullally was caught between the two extremes and seemed pleased to hand over leadership of the gay blessings saga to another bishop later that year.

In 2022 she took part in behind-closed doors discussions to examine the longer-term strategic direction of the C of E. The report this produced, later leaked, recommended the post-pandemic Church cut down its dioceses and bishops to become a slimmed-down missionary organisation. In the end this went nowhere.

Now one of the Church's most senior figures, in 2024 she spearheaded attempts to reform how bishops are selected. Partly due to the divisions unleashed through the battles of gay blessings, meetings of the CNC to appoint new bishops were becoming deadlocked. But Mullally's plans that sought to break the logjam were knocked back by a suspicious synod amid highly-charged debates.

It was as she argued for these reforms that Mullally for once let some of her famous guard down. The bishop broke down into tears as she pleaded with the synod not to kill off a proposed rule guaranteeing female representation on the CNC. Women in the Church, even bishops like her, still regularly experienced 'micro-aggressions', she lamented. Not long before this episode Mullally had also wept as she spoke to her London diocesan synod about the endless trolling and abuse directed at her online.

'She's always deeply embarrassed by that, but actually, you know, she's a human being and it's not a bad thing when it happens,' reflected a senior diocesan official, who said Mullally was also wary that expressions of emotions led to accusations she was trying to manipulate others.

Despite her reputation for reserve, she is universally described as warm, even funny, in private by those who know her well. Throughout her ministry she and her husband Eamonn have enjoyed hosting dinner parties with friends and colleagues. In recent years she has begun to open up in public too. In a podcast interview last year she shared one of her favourite poems (William E. Stafford's 'Ask Me') and her resolute determination to follow where God was calling.

She mused on how guarded she had become in part because she had grown wearily used to people rejecting her ministry because of her gender. A few years ago she had been struck while distributing communion at

St Paul's Cathedral that people were actually happy to receive the eucharist from her for once. 'People aren't always nice to me at the back of church, because I'm a woman and female bishop.' But rather than putting up her defences, she was trying to lean into 'healthy vulnerability'.

As well as rhythms like morning prayer each day at 8 a.m., Mullally enjoys making pottery and tries to go for a jog most days. Eamonn is a passionate pilgrim and serves as trustee of one ancient route which runs from Canterbury to Rome. The last time he walked this, Mullally found the time to join him for parts of the journey. They arrived in Rome just as Pope Francis died in April 2025, allowing her to attend his funeral.

While she is no theological nerd, she has often spoken of how service, both in nursing ('an opportunity to reflect the love of God') and as a priest, is at the heart of her spirituality. Atwell, her former diocesan bishop in Devon, said foot-washing – something she has done literally thousands of times – was the 'defining image' for her as nurse, priest and now bishop.

Being Bishop of London verges on an impossible job in itself, but over the years Mullally's responsibilities have proliferated. Alongside her national Church roles around COVID or LLF, she has also been Dean of the Chapels Royal, an active member of the House of Lords (where she has led the opposition to the assisted dying bill), and chaired the charity Christian Aid. 'She just works and works and works and works,' one colleague said. 'She works like nobody I've ever seen before because her understanding of her calling is absolutely rooted in service. If she's called to do something, she says yes, and she does it to her utmost.'

And so it was no surprise to those who know her when she said yes in October 2025 to becoming the

106th Archbishop of Canterbury. In the build-up to the appointment, Mullally's name was often among the three or four seen as front-runners. And yet her appointment also came as a slight surprise.

She will, of course, be the first woman in the role (which has already antagonised conservative Anglicans elsewhere in the global Anglican Communion). More than that was her age. She will be 64 by the time she takes up the role, leaving her just six years before she hits the mandatory retirement age of 70, and making her, bar one, the oldest archbishop for a century.

But as the archetypal 'safe pair of hands', her accession has made plenty of sense to those who have worked with her. Baines, her first bishop in South London who later worked with her in the Lords, said she had no pretensions about being 'saviour of the world' as archbishop. Instead, her role will be 'getting a grip' on the contentious unresolved issues left behind by Justin Welby, her predecessor. 'That's why she's been appointed: solid, stable,' Baines suggested. 'She has the confidence of the House of Bishops, and that really matters.'

Holtam, the former Bishop of Salisbury said much the same, identifying his one-time protégé as a good 'caretaker' for the Church. Unlike Welby, Mullally was 'completely secure in who she is and competent in what she does'. Her consensual leadership style would help a fractious, squabbling Church come back together again, he predicted.

It was a safeguarding scandal which ultimately did for Welby, and Osborne rejoiced that he was being succeeded by someone she saw as an expert. 'That may sound like the dullest thing an Archbishop of Canterbury can do – it's not saving souls – but it is what the Church of England needs at the moment.'

One of her bishops from London agreed she would focus on 'putting the house in order' once she landed at Lambeth Palace but questioned if she had the vision to go beyond that. The downside of her conciliatory approach to life was that 'nothing actually happens'.

This might be a summation even Mullally herself would not resist. When asked in an interview how she'd approach the daunting task of being archbishop, she responded just like everything else in her career: 'In partnership and collaboration with other people.'

Leading the Church of England was a 'shared ministry', she added, not for heroic lone rangers. 'My experience and my background has been about building good teams of people in healthy cultures. And that's what I bring for this moment, at this time.'

As we go to press

Shortly after Sarah Mullally was announced as the next Archbishop of Canterbury, an old safeguarding case re-erupted and threatened to overshadow her accession. A survivor known only as N had reported their alleged abuse by a London priest years earlier. Unhappy with how this complaint had been handled by Mullally as Bishop of London, they then in 2020 had made a second complaint against her. But due to an administrative foul-up at Lambeth Palace it was not properly processed but instead dropped.

Mullally apologised, although she was not even aware of the second complaint at the time nor responsible for it falling through the cracks, and it was sent off to the Archbishop of York Stephen Cottrell, then in his final weeks as interim head of the C of E. In the lull around Christmas 2025, with Mullally just weeks away from legally becoming Cottrell's de facto boss, he decided there was no case to answer and that his colleague had done nothing wrong in her handling of N's original complaint.

N continued to volubly attack the Church for its supposed re-abuse and victimisation which had caused years of distress and limbo, and his initial accusation of abuse – which the Church had said was fully dealt with at the time – was then re-opened and given to a more junior bishop in London to re-examine.

A handful of clergy in the diocese joined forces with N to demand Mullally's accession to Canterbury be delayed (or even abandoned), but the hierarchy of the Church remained foursquare behind her. Mullally herself made a typically measured statement at the time, agreeing that the Church's processes in handling abuse claims clearly needed strengthening to ensure nobody was left in limbo for years like N. But she insisted she remained the right person to assume leadership of this task as archbishop: 'I will do everything in my power to bring about much-needed and overdue reform. We must have trust in our systems, or else we cannot expect others to put their trust in us.'

1
The Separation of Church and Hate

Spirituality and the Church of England

Mark Oakley

'Unhappy is the land that needs a hero', writes Bertolt Brecht in his play *Life of Galileo*. The current unhappiness that lies deep in parts of the Church of England, matched by similar dissatisfaction with the Church felt in parts of society, means that many are looking for a hero Archbishop of Canterbury to come and rescue us from the tragedy of disappointments that has lately come to define our institution. Whether it is abuse of the vulnerable, decreasing numbers and resources, a lack of leadership, the demise of a plausible voice in the public square, or anger at too much or too little progression in doctrine, liturgy or social justice, the complaints are so loud and mobile that there is a general currency of grievance in circulation which only some superhero, it is tempting to conclude, can ultimately come to rupture and transform.

Such aspiration is flawed with a lack of realism about any one human being's abilities, and with a lack of self-scrutiny as to the part we all play in creating the grievance culture. Any change will only come through a collective will power for it, and the most any Archbishop can do is to help people to recognise this, and to hold the compass as a different path of behaviours is begun. In this regard, any Archbishop today will be working hard in the spirit of St Paul's shepherding and guidance of the earliest Christian communities.

What should an Archbishop be working hard towards, though? A lack of conflict? A greater mutual understanding in those who disagree? A more courageous moral challenge to the world? Or should it be for a more resonant Church for those who are searching for spiritual authenticity and growth? This small contribution I make in this collection of essays is remarkably unoriginal in that it suggests that this last desire should be the first and deepest one in Archbishop Sarah's ministry. I simply argue that it is the soul of the Church, and the longing to keep it healthy and honest, that needs her immediate and long-term focus. The soul of the Church, its 'spirituality', discernible in everything we do and say, locally and nationally, is nothing less than the relationship we have with God.

Our heart lives or fails as a Church as to the quality of attention, or not, we give to this relationship and to what it demands of us in the way we speak of each other and treat each other. It is whether, as a Church, we are interested at all in a deep love of God and deep love of neighbour, or whether we secretly enjoy the shallows, the put down politics, and the unattractive and competitive shaming each other into heaven. Love of God and love of neighbour - totally unoriginal - and yet it feels so urgent somehow. As a Church, just what is the state of our soul? The answer will partly be revealed as to whether we are seen as a flat-tyre community, a spiritually hungry society ironically finding us to be too secular in our preoccupations and conduct, or whether we are offering a persuasive and compelling vision of the Christian life simply by being who we are in Christ. As Evelyn Underhill used to say, at the end of the day the only interesting thing about religion is God.

As the Archbishop begins to think afresh about the state of the Church's soul, I think she would be helped by doing two things – and both involve other heroes of a sort. The first is to go back to what we inherit in our Christian tradition and that has so much wisdom to offer both the Church and society. As a Church we don't live in the past, but we do live with it, and we are offered so much richness for our imagination by those who have lived the Christian life before us. It doesn't surprise me, for instance, that the last two popes before Pope Leo took the names of Benedict and Francis, for these two saints seem to offer the Church, and the world through it, horizons for the human desire of God through their rules of life. Such rules of life, or ways to live a life, are good spiritual practices to encourage in our churches and chaplaincies, coming in many shapes, sizes and traditions. They provide a scaffolding with which to pursue the relationship with God and can help navigate us through such a distracted and distracting landscape. Benedict says they are there to 'safeguard love'. He reminds us of the need for stability in the Christian life, of humility as we live in relationship, and of bowing down to Christ in each other. The silent work of the Benedictines was the leaven for a new civilisation. Francis reminds us equally of the need to let faith breathe in the world, by taking Jesus of Nazareth seriously in his teachings on dependence, possessions, gratitude and the generous heart of the Christ-like. The spirit of Benedict and Francis are needed in the contemporary Church. They both offer visions of Christian discipleship that allow the soul to breathe and expand, when so much anxiety and spiritual sickness does the opposite. If the Church isn't teaching us to love our enemies, but instead keeps telling us who our enemies are, we are not really a Church at all.

I would also be encouraging a new Archbishop to take down the Bonhoeffer volumes from the shelf, and to revisit the saints and martyrs of the twentieth century, from Maria Skobtsova, 'Saint of the Open Door', to Martin Luther King Jr, from Oscar Romero to, in more recent years, Desmond Tutu. I believe dark days lie ahead politically and the Church will be called on to speak up for those who are vulnerable, scapegoated on, or treated as less than human. If we don't, we will have lost our soul to the silence of fear or the cold heart of indifference. We need to be faced again with the cost of discipleship and what the Gospel asks of us. To be learning from those who have stood firm for the values of God's kingdom in recent shadowed and manipulated times, will, I have no doubt, be key to leading the Church over the coming years. 'Piety, piety!', raged Skobtsova, 'but where is the love that moves mountains?'

The second thing an Archbishop might do as a new ministry begins is, as well as being inspirited by the way God has blessed his saints and friends in the past with insight and courage, is to be attentive to the heroes of faith that we have in our own day. I'm talking about the clergy and laity who are working against so many odds, with long hours and an emotional absorption. and projections on them in role, that veer on the inhumane, and who are often taken for granted. Whether they are in city estates, or holding together a large number of rural parishes, or whether they are in chaplaincies amongst those who understand or think little of the Church, or trying to keep a Cathedral alive and standing, volunteering to keep a church open or maintain a food bank, or are trying to initiate a new community that approaches faith from a fresh perspective, there are unsung heroes in the Church, as there are in our local communities, and they need recognising, thanking, and encouraging with a renewed sense of purpose. This is simply a recall to the spiritual discipline of attention and giving thanks. Attention is the beginning of devotion. Faith attends to a God-gifted world that cries out to be seen and cherished. A more significant attending to those who make such sacrifices for the Church's ministry will be a source of deep gratitude and a necessary antidote to the scourge of jaundice that can set in in the Church's culture and, again, paralyses or curdles the soul.

When I occasionally interview women and men discerning whether they are being called to ordained ministry, I often ask them: 'Who do people become in your presence?' Some begin by saying, 'Well, I like to think that x ...'. I stop them. 'No', I say. 'Not what you hope is the case, but, what is the case? What happens to someone when they are with you? What happens to them on the inside?' The same question can be addressed to the Church as an institution. It can also be asked of our leaders. In recent years, the answers will not have been generally positive and, in some cases, they will be deeply shocking. Attending to the people in our midst, recognising what they are doing and at what cost, seeing what life is taking them through and seeking to give them hope and energy for their tasks in that life – all this will be the groundwork for restoring the soul of a Church that comes to enjoy gratitude, not grievance, as its general currency of exchange. It is said that clergy wear clerical collars to show everyone that we are up to our neck in it. It's hard at the moment, exhausting on many levels, for priests and for the lay people who do so much to keep the Church in relationship with localities. The way we treat people as a Church, the tone we set, the detail we take the time to engage with, they all matter. As Maya Angelou reminds us,

'People will forget what you said, people will forget what you did, but people will never forget how you made them feel.'

With refreshed attention to what we should be grateful for in each other, and fortified by the wisdom that is offered us about the Christian life by our forebears, what is it that will ensure we have a healthy soul as a Church? Again, my suggestions are not original. They lie at the heart of the Church of England as I have always understood it. When, at times, that Church has become unrecognisable to me it is usually because I see one of the four vital elements of its being in Christ disappearing from view. When this happens, I sense that I am in a Church of Toyota or Santander, trying to model ourselves on swanky corporates but with less skill and resource. We end up with a Church of 'less than', a Church of pale imitation, and of CEO bishops, with little to make us freshly distinct in a world that needs more significant, alternative, values and relationships to commit to.

The four necessities in our relationship with God as a Church seem to me to be: a renewed confidence in mystery and love, treasuring the poetic and prayerful, seeking to live justly, and renewing our voice by trust and courage. I can only briefly mention these here, but I offer them to our new Archbishop as worthy of a serious but joyful pursuit if we are to keep the soul of the Church of England in good shape for its vocation in society, living only to the glory of God by being here for the common good, and shared life, of the citizens of the nation we are in. We are called to be a thermostat Church, not a thermometer, helping change the temperature, not just taking it. The Church exists not just to make a point but to make a difference. We are ultimately defined not by our past but by what we do next.

The first renewal we might seek is to reclaim

our confidence in love. We say that God is love. We say we believe this. Some theology and decisions we have made in the past and present suggest this not to be the case though. We suggest instead that some love is of God, not all. In some more extreme cases, some Christians even lash out at those whose loving relationships are deemed to be not of God – and nobody hates like a Christian who has just been told that their hate isn't Christian. I am not just urging the Church of England to treat love equally and to celebrate it where two hearts make a commitment – although I am doing that and with some urgency.

I have a fairly simple theology about loving relationships. I believe that if someone is fortunate enough in this life to find someone they love, someone they want to share their life with and grow old with, and look back at their memories one day and say, 'Yes, I was more me because there was us', then the rest of us should do all we can to celebrate and protect them, and as a Church we should be leading the world in believing this and not awkwardly catching up with wider society. I believe this because I do believe that where love is, God is, and that where God is, love is. When someone begins to love God they begin to learn the beauty of a humility and a thankful heart - and they try really hard never to humiliate or shame. This is how a really loving Church would live too. The Church should be a school for learning how to deepen our love, not restrict it. We learn in this school by taking the Bible seriously, and that means living joyfully with the questions it raises as well as the comforts and invitations it brings, but it always means reading the love between its lines and acclaiming Jesus Christ as the Word of God – and when we can't hear the love of God, made visible in him, when someone is talking about the Bible, well, something is up, badly up.

The human soul is born and nurtured by love. As humans we can only be made whole by being loved from the outside and learning to share our love from within. So it is for the Church too, and we will remain less than human, less than humane, if we do not become more confident in the love of God for all those God creates with such tenderness and dignity. Jesus seemed keen to remind us that we can believe all the 'right' things but still be a jerk. It is only by the love we have for each other that people will ultimately know that we are his apprentices. Love defines us, energises us, and will always win – because of God. We must live up to this. Our soul as a Church will always be shadowed until we do.

Because love is never content just to sit in the corner and read, because love has to show itself, the Christian community is sacramental. God is glorious Mystery and mysteries never compromise themselves – instead they reveal themselves, and the revelation leads to an inevitable re-evaluation. Love works mysteriously. Love says life should be like bread shared together and making us even more hungry for God. Love splashes water and says that this is like grace, refreshing our parched ground. Love takes small rings and puts them on the fingers of those who have found themselves in one of life's harbours, and they seal their hearts as metal, hands, hearts, and God all harmonise in a beauty words can't express. Love is sacramental, it gives itself away in signs and miracles, it can't ever just be contained in the head. Everything that matters most we ritualise in, and for, Love. Sacraments embody the grace that relentlessly invite human lives to stop taking small opportunities to be mean and instead take large opportunities to be generous. Love, and love only, is the wonderful conversion from God and to God, and one that brings us all closer in God. The Church I long for is riotously sacramental, with a faith always about beginnings, showing in every sense, and smell, and harmony, and action, that love resurrects everything in the kingdom we belong to. Our spirituality should, in the coming years, be grounded in a renewed celebration and confidence in the wide, and often unsettling, love of God who, every time we draw a line, shows us he is outside it and that we need to keep drawing.

To refresh our soul, too, the Church has to be more confidently poetic, in the sense that when you step into a church you are invited to live in a poem, to inhabit a poem of great beauty and challenge called the Christian faith. The liturgy is poetry in motion, and Christians ought to have a reverence for language in a world that treats it so cheaply. The Church can treat it cheaply too. Harry Williams CR once complained that some new liturgies are 'clumsy constructions in flat, tired English made from assorted pieces of doctrinal Meccano'. We must search for words that war with cliché, that are acrobatic and tease and beguile and surprise. St Paul, in his shepherding of the early Christians, was hugely imaginative as he endlessly searched for images, metaphors and a language that voiced a wonderful conversion of heart that shows the world up for what it has become and the masks it has forced into our faces.

A poetic Church will have to try and be more honest, always more difficult than talking about 'truth', because poetry enters the intellect by way of the heart - so we need to know that human heart well. A poetic Church will also be patient with ambiguity. Poetry resists closure, resists paraphrase, resists the prosaic. And we need to accept the ambiguities of human beings, the fact that they are not knives and forks you fit nicely in compartments, but are always shifting, restless, contradictory and unique – beautiful, in other words, and loved by God for it and not despite it. Our pastors consequently need to be patient. Poetry is a snowfall in the soul and our Christian faith should equally fall like snow around us, showing us the miracle of our breath, our landscape reimagined, the path that now needs to be dug for some spiritual adventure. I pray that God will deliver us, with a new Archbishop, from being a prosaic Church, a Church afraid of poetry and Mystery. I pray that we officiants will not lead worship as if it is a primary school for unimaginative adults, full of childish chatter rather than childlike attentiveness. Rather, our worship should be a space where resonance, the numinous, the hard to imagine or speak about, all press on the heart's experience with a longing to be recognised, cared for, and translated in lives that so often today talk as if we are all much more secular than we really are. The Gospel, like a seed, falls into cracks opened by difficulty and demand, not patronising gimmicks or a dishonest simplicity. There is too much fast-food religion and not enough longer term nutrition around. Such nutrients will only be found in the disciplines of prayer – something, again, that all of us need to be helped with by the Church – that is, by each other. The praying of Morning and Evening Prayer alone or in company is vital to the soul of the Church's ministry and yet often gets pushed out by the diary or never understood to be necessary even. An Archbishop of Canterbury will need to be unapologetic about the need for prayer in her own life, and seek to help others discover its strength and distillation.

I also long for a Church that is just, that takes social justice to be of God, that sees the dignity in each human being to be of God, that never allows compassion to replace what is just because, frankly, it is easier. Without justice there cannot be love, it is the social form of the love we celebrate, nothing less. We all kneel, we all get a piece of the same bread, we are all loved equally and then told to go with peace in our hearts to love and serve the Lord. How? By reflecting what has been done to us. This is a hard world where, it has been said, if you are not at the table you are probably on the menu. In the eucharist, though, we are all at the table and, as George Herbert knew, love takes all our hands smiling, lifting us up so we can have our full stops turned into commas, and then freed to go and do the same for those who need their dignity to be reclaimed. The faith of the Church is a loving search into the mystery of God but it is also God's searching love for us, searching us out in our hurt and need, and when in place and ready, telling us to go and do likewise. In his encyclical *Dilexi te*, Pope Leo argues that 'doctrinal rigour without mercy is empty talk' and that the Church's deepest vocation is to love the Lord 'where he is most disfigured'. 'When the Church bends down to care for the poor', he concludes, 'she assumes her highest posture.' We need such teaching from the Church of England, not with a synodical tone, but with a celebration that we mean what we say and will show it. This is the only way to ensure our soul as a Church is authentic.

Too many times the Church has preferred to be an example of power rather than live the power of example. We do well to remember the funeral rite of Habsburg royalty at which the glorious funeral procession, full of pomp, led its way to the capuchin convent where the imperial chapel resides. On arrival the doors were found to be shut. The Grand Chamberlain knocked on the door three times and the voice of the Abbot from inside the church was heard: 'Who is it?' The Chamberlain then read out all the long and many grand titles of the deceased, the Archduke of this, the Grand Duke of that. At the end, the voice said: 'We know him not'. The Chamberlain knocked again. 'Who is it?' came the voice. And this time, the Chamberlain reduced the titles to their bare minimum, just three or four. 'We know him not', came the reply. Three more knocks. 'Who is it?' 'A sinner in need of God's mercy' says the Chamberlain. The voice was heard from the church. 'Him we know, enter.' And the doors were opened. It is only with this truth about the Christian community, that we are sinners in need of mercy, that the poetic faith begins its story about us and in us. The challenges for the Church at the moment are many, and the task of the Archbishop is unforgiving and unenviable. If, however, she can help us look again at our soul, at our inner life that defines our identity and potential, as a Church, and at the ways in which it is seen and felt to be for the common good, by both neighbours and nation, then the years will be well spent.

There is a word that has only been recorded once in the Oxford English Dictionary – 'respair'. It means fresh hope, a recovery from despair. It is my heartfelt hope that, with the companionship of a new Archbishop, we can bring that respair to our Church and to our world with a recovery of soul.

PRAYER

Philip Larkin, the poet who wrote of the 'million petalled flower of being here', once wrote to a priest in Hull after attending evensong and benediction. 'I bow my head', he wrote, 'at what you do, and raise it again at the manner in which you do it.' I'll be praying that the world may say the same of the Church one day because of our confidence in love, our embrace of Mystery, our courage for justice, and our belief that human relationships need schooling by the beauty and wisdom of our Lord given on the mountain of Beatitude, and by the saints of God who took him at his word. In the words of St John Chrysostom, 'God does not need golden vessels, but golden souls.'

2
Facing Truth With Honesty

Nationalism, Racism and the Church of England

Eileen Harrop

Introduction

A new season has begun for the Church of England ('the Church') as Archbishop Sarah Mullally takes office; a season marked by profound need and opportunity, ripe for renewed ministry and mission, across the nation. The Church is the Established Church with a spiritual voice in the UK Parliament[1] and, although the place of the Lords Spiritual in the upper house is debated, the nation expects Christian leadership of the Church. In this season, the Church's commitment to dismantling institutional racism meets a nation wrestling with English nationalism and British identity, with sharp disagreements over immigration, asylum seekers and refugees. In this context, Archbishop Sarah will hear opposing voices, some welcoming encouragement from the Church's stance, others hopeful that the Church would provide spiritual foundation for their political positions.

This chapter sets out the call on Archbishop Sarah to keep the Church rooted in the Good News that is in Christ, to site race, identity, and nationalism according to God's Kingdom as revealed in the Gospels and by the testimony of prophets, leaders, and disciples in the Bible. The people in and of this nation reasonably hopes for this from the Church's Christian leadership. The basis for all action must be the Christian message, reminding the nation that God's created humanity of all races, every ethnicity, tribes and nations, has shared identity in the one body in Christ.

In Christ, we sing '*a new song, saying, "Worthy are you to take the scroll and to open its seals, for you were slain, and by your blood you ransomed people for God from every tribe and language and people and nation"*' (Revelation 5:9 English Standard Version (ESV); that Christians are to '*clothed (y)ourselves with Christ. There is neither Jew nor Greek, slave nor free, male nor female, for (you) we are all one in Christ Jesus*' (Galatians 3:27-28 ESV).

The Church's teaching on how we are to regard and treat one another is clear, and it must be reflected in our common life. Where discrepancies are uncovered between this calling and our institutional practice, the nation expects from the Church no prevarication and no excuses in putting matters right.

In what follows, we do three things. First, we trace the deep roots of English identity, Empire, and the Church's complicity in racial injustice. Second, we examine the current moment in which economic deprivation, populist nationalism, and cuts to racial justice funding risk pulling the Church away from its professed commitments. Third, we turn to the missionary calling of Christ and the gifts of Global Majority Heritage ('GMH') Christians, asking how Archbishop Sarah might lead a Church that embodies the Kingdom's multi-ethnic, justice-seeking life in this land.

In the legacy of the British Empire, many people in this nation are voicing longing for identity and local rootedness. In response, some politicians are framing an English nationalist agenda that is exclusionary, nostalgic, and hostile, stoking fears of change to

English culture, and blaming migrants and GMH communities for social and economic problems.

In recent years, the Church, revisiting the history of slavery and its complicity in injustices stemming from decisions made during the British Empire, is taking ownership of its part in the consequential institutional racism of the Church's practices, structures and culture.

This chapter reflects on where we are as a nation and Church. Are we taking the lead to be racially aware and just, and offering a faithful and generous vision of national identity? We draw on the insights of the Anglican Minority Ethnic Network ('AMEN') – the ethnocultural network established to come alongside the Church as 'a critical friend' as well as to challenge the Church on behalf of its United Kingdom Minority Ethnic ('UKME') and GMH laity and clergy on matters of Racism and Racial Justice. We consider how the Church might speak prophetically to the anxieties and fractures of our age while modelling a community shaped by the courageous and reconciling love of Christ. We look to the Church's renewed witness of the Kingdom of God, with deeper commitment to justice, representation, and hospitality, that influences the shaping of identity of people in this nation.

The chapter considers other concerns such as socio-economic deprivation, which some politicians have weaponised to promote a racist nationalism. In 2023 and 2024, AMEN intentionally formed partnerships with the United Society Partners in the Gospel ('USPG') and the Church Urban Fund ('CUF'), recognising that socio-economic health and global Christian mission are integral to the national identity and flourishing of this nation.

As Archbishop Sarah begins her new ministry, we call on her to lead a Church that faces truths with honesty, denouncing misuse of Christian identity, and affirming the multi-racial, multi-national, multi-cultural, and multi-heritage design of God's Kingdom. She is well-placed to lead a Church whose members and participants exemplify loving God and loving one another, guiding this nation into a future where every person finds dignity in compassion, belonging, and hope.

History

The English national identity is steeped in Anglo-Saxon history before the British Empire, and honed since then; characterised by global travel and endeavour, territorial conquests, invention, and industrialisation. Throughout this shaping of identity, the Church, through missionary activity, influence on public life, and alignment with the Crown and government, has been woven into the fabric of imperial history and its legacies.

Righteousness and justice are the foundation of your throne; steadfast love and faithfulness go before you. (Psalm 89:14 ESV)

Unlike the Psalmist's declaration, not all our imperial legacy testifies to God's righteousness. We did not always deal justly with others. We did not always respond with the love and peace of Christ to the welcome of indigenous hosts, nor did we always consider our faithfulness to God's commandments. Territorial conquests, victorious by the political designs and measures of the British Empire, were far from victorious by the measure of *'loving our neighbour as ourselves'*. There is nothing Christian in the imposition of authority and domination over peoples, to enslave them and dishonour their human dignity. The gains from conquests and enslavement are ill-gotten, theft not only of property but of lives belonging to God the Father and Creator. These are not realities on which a nation guided by the Church would wish to build national identity.

The legacy of these injustices did not end when the Empire waned. When the Commonwealth of Nations was formed as Britain relinquished authority over countries in its Empire, an attitude of superiority and entitlement has lingered and shaped this nation's prevailing culture. We call on Archbishop Sarah to guide this nation in transition, wrestling to embrace a future that includes people of GMH, of many colours, races, ethnicities, and the evolving cultural diversity.

Church Commissioners have admitted that the Church's historic wealth is partly built on investments linked to transatlantic slavery.[2] The Church has acknowledged the injustices faced by those invited from the Empire's dominions and colonies to help rebuild post-war Britain and of those called from former colonies to assist its armed forces in the World Wars and in subsequent military tours. Instead of the welcome and support they were promised and gratitude for their sacrificial response, many met racial discrimination, were denied their legal rights and, in many cases, wrongly treated as illegal immigrants, neither recognised nor rewarded equitably for their service to the nation. For too long the Church has been ambivalent, failing as the Established Church to speak against the ill-treatment and gross injustice towards them.

In 2020, the Church's General Synod issued a formal apology for racism experienced by Black and Minority Ethnic Anglicans ('BAME'), victims and families of victims, of the Windrush Scandal, and in 2023 established a £100 million fund to address this legacy of slavery.[3] These acknowledgements, whilst welcomed, point to a wider pattern in which communities who have suffered injustice still find the Church slow to act on their behalf.

During the Industrial Revolution, the Church was a major landowner in receipt of significant income from royalties and rents derived from the coal and lead mines on their land. The Church's visible support for the livelihoods and plight of mining communities during the 1926 lock out and the Miners' Strike of the mid-1980s, is an example of courageous leadership that softened the Church's reputation as the 'employer class' and as an echo chamber for the government of the day. During the mid-1980s Miners' Strikes, several senior clergy including the Archbishop of Canterbury The Most Revd Robert Runcie, who commissioned the 1985 *Faith in the City* Report, and the Bishop of Durham The Rt Revd David Jenkins, were highly vocal against the government's policies and actions that would drive many communities into poverty.[4]

'The long seven-month lockout of 1926 was to be a time when conflicting symbols and ideologies battled for dominance and men and women had to prioritise their values and act upon them. The success of the parish priests in presenting their churches as (at the very least) apolitical bodies, allowed strikers to avoid any potential conflict between their religious and their political beliefs, and meant that the church was able to maintain its standing in the region'.[5]

Today, communities struggling to rise from deprivation, are being politically manipulated to direct blame for their plight onto migrants and GMH people.

The Revd Jon Swales has poetically described the sense of loss, the wrestling with hope, in such communities:

East of Eden: Gateshead

The Angel of the North
rusted, enormous,
stands watch over broken estates.

Not protection.
A witness.

Revd Pam walks the cut
towards the youth worker's flat.
Grey drizzle.
Bin bags spilling.
Shouting from upstairs windows.

Trained at St Hild near Leeds,
cut her teeth in a suburban curacy,
but felt the call North,
to where the Angel spreads its arms.

She passes Kenny,
voice like gravel,
eyes red from Stella.
'Church lot divvent knaa, pet,' he mutters,
'kids roond here haven't a chance.'
Then he half-laughs, shakes his head.
'Got sanctioned again.
Nee leccy.
Gonna have to kip in me coat.'

She keeps walking.
Sarah pushes a pram,
cigarette clamped between her teeth.
'The bairn's da?
Back inside.
Scrappin'.
Probation means nowt.'
She shrugs, smoke curling.
'Aye well, Father Christmas divvent come te Gateshead.'

Pam reaches the youth worker.
Alicia.

Mid-twenties.
Brilliant, fierce, but tired,
shoulders slumped.
She's carrying a box.
Files, notebooks, a mug.

'I can't do it, Pam.
Every door –
stuff I can't scrub out me head.
Last week – dad.
Shed.
Rope.
Kids screaming.
Mum done in.

And then that lad –
hunters on his step,
camera in his face,
all over bloody Facebook before a judge sees him.
Paint on his door: PEDO.
Neighbours spitting.
He don't sleep. Shakes all night.

I can't.
I'm not strong.
I thought I was.
But this place – it eats you.'

Pam wants to hold her,
but just nods.
'Of course you can't.'
She sees vicarious trauma in Alicia's face,
the haunted look she's known in herself.

She thinks: I could pay,
for counselling,
From my own pocket.

Facing Truth With Honesty

The PCC's skint,
but I've still got some savings.

She doesn't say it.
Keeps it inside.

Alicia shakes her head.
'It's not the job, Pam.
It's the world.
And it's crushing me.'
She presses the keys into Pam's palm.

Pam breathes deep.
She thinks of ordination vows,
oil on skin,
sent to bring gospel to the poor.
But gospel feels thin here –
stretched till it tears.
A voice in her chest snarls:
Where the hell are you, God?

That night she phones her sister in Oxford.
Recruitment firm.
Big house.
Kitchen island.
Wine poured into crystal.

'How's parish life?' her sister asks.
Pam hesitates.
Does she speak of Alicia broken?
Of children hungry?
Of the Angel standing over estates
where hope rusts?

Her sister carries on,
talks of ski trips,
pupil premiums at private schools,

the au pair who keeps burning the risotto.
Then she laughs:
'You'd love it here –
we're fundraising for the prep school bursary.
Making sure even less fortunate children can ski.'

Pam listens.
Says nothing.

Later,
in the cold church,
she kneels beneath the crucifix.
She thinks of Jesus saying,
'Let the children come to me.'
She thinks of James:
'If a brother or sister lacks food
and you say, "Keep warm,"
but give them nothing,
what is the good of that?'

And then she remembers:
Jesus blessed the poor,
lifted the hungry,
turned tables for the broken.
But he also said,
'Take up your cross.
Follow me.'
Not cheap words,
but blood and surrender.
Bias to the poor,
but cost to the disciple.

Pam weeps.
Not for answers,
but for the weight she can't lay down,
the ache of a gospel
that demands everything

and still feels too small
for Gateshead's grief.

So she prays —
not for fire that burns her out,
not for zeal that consumes and collapses,
but for love that lasts.
Sustainable love.
The kind that steadies,
endures,
does not fail.

No wonder Jesus sent them out in pairs,
she thinks.
But Alicia has gone.
No other workers.
Just her,
a hollow rectory,
and a congregation already stretched.
She'll advertise for a replacement —
but knows the post may never be filled.
Only six months left on the grant.

And the other church —
the one with the SDF money,
brimming with staff,
Instagram worship nights,
but the poor left outside the door.
She tries not to be jealous.
Tries.

Yet she knows, too,
the grit of her parishioners,
the stubborn humour,
the Geordie warmth.
Every visit,
always the offer of a cuppa —

no matter how little in the cupboard.
Once she heard a lass who'd offered her tea
nip next door, whisper for a teabag,
then come back smiling,
mug in hand,
hospitality unbroken.

Even here,
among mould and hunger,
there are glimmers.
Last Sunday –
a family baptised.
Dad found faith in prison,
came out new,
married the mother of his children.
Now four kids in the pews,
wide-eyed,
singing hallelujah with crisp packets crackling.
The Spirit still falls in Gateshead,
just as Joel promised,
'on sons and daughters,
on young and old,
even on the least.'

The Angel spreads its iron arms,
east of Eden.
Wings heavy with witness,
but also with hope.
Children still hungry.
Workers still broken.
Empire still grinding.
And yet –
a compass points to the wounded Christ,
where bread is broken,
water poured,
and even in Gateshead,
God is not absent.

When the Church speaks into both issues as matters of justice, for communities troubled by anxieties of economic degradation and for racially diverse GMH and UKME people, its Christian leadership promotes cohesion and nullifies divisiveness.

Christian faith does not require the erasure of national identity. Love of place, language, story, and landscape can be a gift, part of what it means to seek the welfare of the city where God has placed every person. The Gospel testifies against racialised nationalism that defines belonging as exclusion of newcomer and stranger. When 'Englishness' is imagined as white, monocultural, and under threat, and when Christian language is deployed to defend that imagination, the Church must say clearly that such nationalism is idolatry rather than discipleship. Our baptismal identity in Christ is the reference for all other identities, however valued, and calls us into a community gathered from *'every tribe and language and people and nation'* (Revelations 5:9 ESV).

The Church Today

The Archbishop of York, The Rt Revd Stephen Cottrell, reported that *'progress towards racial justice in the Church of England has been slow – painfully slow'*, and *'we are still far from where we want to be, where we need to be, as a Church'* (*Church Times*, 24 July 2025). Yet the Church Commissioners have announced that the £20 million fund allocated to racial justice work in the 2023-25 triennium is 'a one-off'. The new triennium 2026 to 2028 funding allocation of £7 million with £200,000 carried over from the previous triennium funds for 'social and racial justice' is a composite fund that includes housing and disability justice. It is obvious that social justice and racial justice warrant increased not decreased funding if divisive, politically-loaded nationalism is not to escalate.

Because the Church's decisions demonstrate its seriousness about living justly, we urge Archbishop Sarah to respond to such overt discrepancies between what the Church says and what it actually does.

National identity, Englishness, and the legacy of the British Empire are intrinsically interwoven. Mass immigration and the entry of people of multiple ethnicities are outworkings of the British Empire and its reach across continents east and west. The Empire has come home, even if settled communities in 'the mother country' had not been adequately prepared to extend Christian welcome. The Church has the opportunity to show how this nation can take responsibility, by Christian example, for our actions.

'You shall have the same rule for the sojourner and for the native, for I am the Lord your God.' (Leviticus 24:22, NIV)

(Jesus said) 'Whoever has two tunics is to share with him who has none, and whoever has food is to do likewise.' (Luke 3:11, ESV)

We are a Christian country, whose Sovereign is the Supreme Governor of the Church. It is always timely to show Christian leadership in this nation's welcome to those who are invited and those who sojourn here.

While it is not the Church's role to define 'Englishness' or national identity, it is the Church's role to lead by its own example of Christian love and how people are to treat one another.

(Jesus said) 'A new commandment I give to you, that you love one another: just as I have loved you, you also are to love one another. By this all people will know that you are my disciples, if you have love for one another.' (John 13:34-35)

Recent events show how the Church cannot be bystanders. Political protests in which crosses, Bible verses, and chants of '*Christ is King*' have been used to present racialised visions of Christianity, of 'God, faith, family, homeland.'[6] The Church cannot be silent when symbols of Christ are raised against asylum seekers and minority communities.

The Missionary Calling of Christ

Ordained Ministry in the Church is the response of Christians called by God to this vocation in the Church, even as Christ called Peter to build the Church.

As Christians from this country once heard God's call to journey to distant lands, particularly during the era of the British Empire, to share the Good News and make disciples of all nations, so too has God called people from other nations to bring the Gospel to the people of this land.

The fervour, conviction, commitment, and experience of church growth that many Spirit-filled GMH Christians bring to ordained ministry here ought to be celebrated. At a time when declining attendance in the Church is a concern, this should be a source of profound encouragement. Yet first-hand reports show that too often their vocation is not acknowledged. Instead, they are frequently met with guarded judgement and subjected to more stringent evaluation than their peers.

This disparity is reflected in the wider Anglican Communion. While ordained ministers from the Church are welcomed and readily licensed to serve elsewhere in the Communion, those from the wider Communion do not find the open welcome reception here. Many find themselves excluded from incumbent roles, and even bishops from the wider Communion can be treated as candidates required to justify their episcopal call and suitability for vacant Sees. At present, there are no consistent pathways that fully acknowledge the vocations, experience, and leadership of those GMH clergy and senior ministers.

UKME and GMH Anglicans are scrutinised for every characteristic – colour, ethnicity, race, language, culture; and those who are Minority and GMH women often have added scrutiny; which may be counted against their suitability, deployability, for ministry roles at all levels. Their vocational discernment includes confronting institutional barriers, including the bias of some senior bishops and leaders in the National Church Institution (NCI). Due to the increased political outcry against migrants, GMH Anglicans who have discerned the call to Ordained Ministry here are subject to the same policies used to sift out the unwelcome alien. Many called to serve in England come in their mature years with proven leadership in corporate, professional, and church life. But the Church has for more than a decade been lowering the age for Ordinands sponsored for full-time training and stipendiary ministry. The current cut off at 40 counts against GMH candidates, many having spent longer in higher education and in professional lay occupations. The Church has made no provision for GMH candidates who would have given up their professional lives abroad, requiring them to secure employment in this nation's environment, which is hostile to migrant workers.

The Church has been compelled to improve its understanding, ownership, governance, policies and practices for safeguarding people against abuse of children and vulnerable adults. Due to the prevalence of racism in the Church, UKME and GMH laity and clergy are more vulnerable to being bullied, excluded, and on the receiving end of passive-aggressive behaviours, than others, without the Church's institutional protection or recourse when abused.[7] The Charity Commission has highlighted this restrictive safeguarding arrangement as inadequate, because abuse against all adults is unacceptable. It is apposite for Archbishop Sarah to lead the Church into safeguarding UKME and GMH laity and clergy against abuse and injustice.

We know that the Church can set its mind to removing these institutional barriers. Archbishop Sarah, the Archbishops Council, the Church Commissioners, the House of Bishops, and General Synod, can at least address institutional racism with the same urgency and attention as their collective response to the George Floyd murder and subsequent support for the 'Lament to Action Task Force' and its recommendations.[8]

It is inconsistent for the Church to go along with the Government's discriminatory policies that deny legitimate entry and support for people called by Christ to minister in this land. Where there is political will, there is a way. After all, does not the Windrush scandal testify to this?

Hopes for the leadership of Archbishop Sarah

The people in England are hungry for the Church's spiritual leadership. Although not to be conflated with moral leadership, there is deep hope that the Church would show moral courage in proclaiming the Good News of Christ, that what she practises by example would duly influence the Government as befits its role as the Established Church. Have the Lords Spiritual been reactive to issues debated in Parliament and the Church therefore seen to be imbalanced in speaking on matters deemed political rather than spiritual?

We encourage Archbishop Sarah to lead the Church into a new period when institutional racism is dismantled; of affirming the missionary people of the Global Majority world called to serve in the Church here; and to direct the nation's attention to the Church's faithfulness and confidence to live out the Good News of Jesus Christ, of Righteousness and Justice for a nation of diverse people in Kingdom of God.

AMEN as the independent umbrella ethnocultural network representing UKME and GMH laity and clergy is ready to assist Archbishops Mullally and Cottrell as they lift up this nation in the righteous and just leadership of Christ.[9]

[1] https://researchbriefings.files.parliament.uk/documents/CBP-8886/CBP-8886.pdf
[2] https://www.churchofengland.org/about/governance/national-church-institutions/church-commissioners-england/who-we-are/church-commissioners-links-african-chattel-enslavement
[3] https://www.churchofengland.org/sites/default/files/2024-03/church-commissioners-for-england-oversight-group-report-to-the-board-of-governors.pdf
[4] https://www.chpublishing.co.uk/books/9780715143261/faith-in-the-city and The Rt Revd David Jenkins was quoted in the House of Parliament as saying at His Enthronement as Bishop of Durham, 'the miners must not be defeated. They are desperate for their communities and this desperation forces them to action' https://hansard.parliament.uk/commons/2024-05-09/debates/A39CED0F-9C1E-4F44-84A9-C5ED4B6953D8/MinersAndMiningCommunities
[5] Twentieth Century British History, Volume 17, Issue 3, 2006, Pages 350–372, https://doi.org/10.1093/tcbh/hwl019
[6] https://www.theguardian.com/commentisfree/2025/aug/24/flag-hard-right-prejudice-england
[7] https://www.research.ed.ac.uk/en/publications/if-it-wasnt-for-god-a-report-on-the-wellbeing-of-global-majority-
[8] https://www.churchofengland.org/media/press-releases/lament-action-archbishops-anti-racism-taskforce-calls-urgent-changes-culture
[9] With thanks to AMEN's Vice Chair, Revd Dr Godfrey Kesari; Secretary Samuel Williams; and Treasurer John Tasker for their inputs to the writing of this chapter
[10] With thanks to the Archdeacon of Halifax, The Venerable Bill Braviner, a member of AMEN

PRAYER[10]

Hear our prayer, Lord,
for your servant Sarah,
as her hands are placed
at the helm of your church;
may you be the compass of her soul
ever leading her to your love,
that with you as her pilot
she may be blessed
with wisdom and grace,
in welcoming and valuing
all who bear your image;
with commitment and courage
to work for justice and reconciliation;
to lead and guide your people
on the course you set before us,
that together we may share
the healing and hope
of your gospel and kingdom
that your righteousness and justice
be found
in one another,
in our nation,
and in all the world,
to the glory of your name.
Amen.

3
A Place for All Bodies

Welcoming and empowering disabled people in the Church of England

Emily Richardson

The Christian faith is body-positive. Every Christmas we celebrate a baby being born: a human baby who cried, felt hunger and pain, grew up in a human family and became a man who experienced the breadth of our shared existence. And we affirm in our creeds that *that* man was in fact the second person of the Trinity: God incarnate. In my most difficult moments, when my body has seemed to me to be broken, a source of pain and something I have wanted to escape from, I have returned to the fact that bodies matter enough to God for him to have chosen to inhabit one. This can be a source of comfort and sometimes even a source of frustration.

Sadly, we live in a society where not all bodies are valued as equal. There are ideals of bodies: normative examples of what they should be able to achieve and produce or how they should look and behave. Bodies and minds that diverge from the norm are seen to be difficult, and as such aren't always accommodated with the ease and dignity they deserve. This is a time of structural injustice against disabled and neurodivergent people - we call it *ableism*. This is a time when we are told, in the words of Disability Justice activists Stacey Milbern and Patty Berne, that 'some bodies [and minds] are valuable and some are disposable'.[1]

It is not an easy time to be a disabled, chronically ill or neurodivergent person. It never has been, of course, but things feel particularly challenging at the moment. At the most recent St Martin-in-the-Fields/Inclusive Church Disability Conference,[2] we chose wilderness as a theme because for many disabled people, that is where we find ourselves. With threatened cuts to disability benefits, an NHS under strain and rising political and social tension, we can feel particularly vulnerable. We are easy targets for blame and scapegoating, and yet in reality we often have to deal with a degrading benefits system to get the most basic support. According to disability charity Scope, disabled people are almost twice as likely to be unemployed as non-disabled people and can face up to £975 a month in extra costs.[3] More than a quarter of disabled people experience food insecurity in the UK.[4] In today's cost-of-living crisis, more and more disabled people are choosing not just between heating and eating, but between eating and powering life-saving medical equipment. This is maybe why the wilderness metaphor resonated so strongly with many of us.

Sadly, the Church is not immune to wider society's influences and can often be a wilderness for disabled Christians rather than a comfort. In 2022, I co-wrote *At the Gates* with Dr Naomi Lawson Jacobs, based on Naomi's PhD research with disabled people on their experiences of church. We encountered a wide range of experiences: some positive, others less so.

The resounding question from our storytellers was: 'Why is the Church not speaking out against disability injustice? Where is the Church that preaches about a Christ *who came for* marginalised people *before* he came for the rich and powerful?'

Fiona MacMillan is the chair of the Disability Advisory Group at St Martin-in-the-Fields Church in London, a disabled-led ministry. In *At the Gates* she told us, 'The disability work at St Martin's began in 2011 when, amidst wider austerity, the Church of England cut its own funding for work with disabled people ... At a time of fear and anxiety at government policy and rising disability hate crime, there was a sense that disabled people, already excluded in terms of access and participation, were even further excluded from the Church – the one place which you'd hope would speak up and act. This became a catalyst for our disability work at St Martin's – because if not us, then who?'

In July 2022, I was watching the livestream of General Synod when my sister asked me what they were debating. 'Well, this is a debate on the inclusion and affirmation of disabled people within the life of the church.' She looked somewhat confused and asked, 'Do you mean to say they don't do that already?' It was hard to know how to answer that question honestly.

Of course, disability inclusion in the Church has moved on a lot and as a disabled person I can say that I feel part of the Church in many ways. During the social reforms of the Victorian period, the church was at the forefront of caring for and supporting those on the margins. This was what may be called a *charity model* of disability. We were primarily the objects of care and ministry. Other models of disability include the *medical model:* bodies are reduced to conditions or impairments needing to be fixed. They are to be treated, fixed and the goal is always to get the person back to the closest version of normal that can be achieved. For a lot of my life, I have unwittingly placed myself within that model - always seeking the latest opinion or new treatment.

It wasn't until I discovered the *social model* of disability that I began to rethink my whole attitude to my body and how I treated her. The social model insists that it is *society* that disables the person. When access needs are denied or accommodations are not met, people are denied full participation. We are disabled by architecture, design and, perhaps most of all, by people's attitudes.

These attitudes create damage to how disabled people are perceived. Our inclusion is sometimes framed as an act of kindness and charity rather than a matter of equal belonging and rights. We are seen primarily as recipients of care rather than as active members or leaders within the Church. More concerningly, there are underlying theological ideas that can often underpin attitudes to disability, particularly the historic connection between disability and sin and the insistence on healing.

As we welcome a new Archbishop of Canterbury, we acknowledge that we are in a wilderness when it comes to disability and access. Thankfully, we know that God has a special affinity for the wilderness. It's where he does all of his best work. We know, as Christians, that there is hope in the wilderness if you are attuned to the ways of God. So what are some of those beacons of hope?

Start with ramps ... but don't end there

As I have attended conferences and seminars on disability and the church, I've often heard the phrase 'it's not just ramps and hearing loops'. The conversation around disability and Church is not just about physical access. But of course, it is a fundamental starting point for any considerations about inclusion and justice for disabled people in the Church. If people cannot get into the building or interpret and understand the service then that is a fundamental failure to serve and minister to people in your congregation.

Disabled Christians, like many of those who we featured in *At the Gates*, require many different kinds of access. There are physical access needs, like getting into buildings and accessing facilities like toilets or reaching the altar at communion. There are sensory access needs, particularly for those who find some aspects of our liturgies difficult to navigate. There are auditory and visual access needs, for those who cannot read service sheets or cannot hear the words of those leading. These are all really important barriers which we need to address and tackle. Thankfully, there are resources and ideas to share in our churches and congregations. Disabled people very quickly learn to be problem-solvers: we often can provide simple solutions or recommendations to barriers.

One of the main issues we found was that provision of access was often limited to the pews. It was not even considered that other parts of the church would need to be accessible: the pulpit and the altar, for example. Disabled people were seen to be recipients in church, not part of the ministry team or leadership. This is an attitude that we desperately need to address if the Church is going to be a place of justice and flourishing for all members of the Body of Christ.

Embrace incarnation

One of the theological motifs that many of our storytellers found to be transformative in their understanding of God was the idea of the Disabled God.[5] If we fail to embrace and celebrate disability within our community we are missing out on a vital aspect of the personhood of God.

Central to our faith is a broken body, a body disabled and disfigured. The prophet Isaiah speaks of the suffering servant, despised and rejected. This body is not the perfect, strong figure that our society celebrates and glorifies. It is weak and vulnerable, powerless and dependent. And although this body is restored – resurrection does not destroy the body – when it does reappear, it does so with scars intact. In fact, it is a central part of the resurrected Jesus, the holes in his hands and side, are how the disciples know for sure that it is him. These 'glorious scars' as the hymn-writer calls them, are not erased in Christ's death, but carried into his new life, even celebrated.

To be human is to be vulnerable and to be part of the Church is to embrace that vulnerability. In the Gospels we have a saviour who is not afraid of expressing and modelling that vulnerability. Many of the disabled people we interviewed were denied full inclusion in their churches because of a perceived lack, and yet we are taught in scripture God using what is weak to shame the strong (1 Corinthians 1:27). Could it be that we have something vital to teach the Church?

Heed the prophets

The disability theologian John Hull said, 'Disabled people have a distinct ministry in the church. Disabled people are not so much a pastoral problem as a prophetic potential. We need to ask not how the church can care for disabled people but to ask what is the prophetic message of the church in our culture and how disabled people can make a unique contribution to that renewal.'[6]

When I think of prophets I think of the outcasts. Prophets in the Bible don't have the best reputation for being popular. They do not win friends and influence people, at least not in the way the world sees. Think back to Moses, ministering to a wandering people, Jeremiah and Ezekiel, enduring the social and physical hardships that come with having to speak truth to power. Jonah was so delighted with his mission that he ran in the opposite direction. Prophets stand on the edge and reflect the injustices of their community back to them. They challenge, accuse, argue, provoke, like the irritating piece of grit in the oyster. Over and over they insist to whoever is willing to listen to them that another way is possible.

Disabled Christians continue in that tradition. We wrote *At the Gates* hoping to capture some of that prophetic potential that John Hull called us to embody. We set out to record the voices of the outsiders at the gates, calling for greater justice. The seeds for renewal, change and greater justice for all of God's kingdom are sown on the edge. We need the Church and its leaders to listen to them.

Invest in Leadership

I have found Diocesan Disability Advisors to be a vital resource in enabling dioceses to become more disability-confident. DDAs aim to promote disability issues within their dioceses, through educating and training clergy and laity in issues of disability and neurodiversity. At present most dioceses have a named DDA, but there is no parity across the board. Only four dioceses have paid positions and many DDAs take on the position as part of a wider diversity brief. There is an active network of DDAs who support one another in their roles, however, DDAs currently have no training for the role, so one challenge is a lack of consistency in knowledge and experience.

Some of the storytellers we spoke to had navigated their own journeys in ministry within the Church. There were a range of experiences, from those who had entered the vocations process and been supported and encouraged to those who had faced continued barriers within ministry. As church buildings are often built with healthy people in mind, so our models of ministry and training often expect normative roles and expressions of 'what a minister looks like'. We expect disabled people to fit into structures and systems that are not designed for them, rather than listening to their experiences and using them to shape and change the way we do things. Initiatives such as the neurodiversity training programme in the Diocese of London have been successful in resourcing our leaders. Investment in DDAs and improvement of the way we train our leaders is one way that we can do this: modelling culture change begins in our structures and values. Only then, with the help of the Spirit, it trickles down into our parishes and communities.

Transform culture

Ultimately, we are seeking to create a culture of accessibility, one that informs practical provision of access but also overhauls our *attitudes* around issues of which bodies are valued and challenges that ableism that unfortunately has leaked into our churches from surrounding culture. Scripture reminds us that we are all fearfully and wonderfully made. In fact that is the basis of the Synod motion on disability in July 2022:

> 'This Synod, affirming disabled people (with hidden as well as visible disabilities) to be fearfully and wonderfully made in the image and likeness of God, and mindful of the progress already made in removing some of the barriers which disabled people, clergy and lay, face; commit to working towards the removal of all remaining barriers to full participation for disabled people in the life and ministry of the church.'[7]

Disabled theologian Dr Amy Kenny has said that growing up she 'had the audacity to believe the Psalmist's claim'[8] and it can sometimes feel audacious to live as a disabled person in the church. To believe that the image of God is broad enough to reflect the diversity of bodies and minds that exist in creation. Disabled Christians need to hear from pulpits and those in leadership that this really *is* the belief of the church. That 'we have a new dignity' as the baptismal prayer affirms to each child of God.

There is another dimension to consider in the coming years, as the Assisted Dying Bill is debated in the UK Parliament. This is a practical example of how our views and assumptions can have real-world consequences. At the time of writing there are conversations taking place around legalising assisted dying which are indeed complex and invoke a wide range of reactions within and outside of the Church. Archbishop Sarah has already spoken about the dangerous message already creeping into some of the arguments. 'If passed, this Bill will signal that we are a society that believes that some lives are not worth living.'[9] Proposed laws are seemingly reinforcing the hierarchy of bodies and minds that ableism seeks to uphold: *this is disability theology!* Listening to the voices of disabled people and taking their concerns seriously is vital in the current climate.

It is often remarked that the disabled community is the only minority that anyone can be welcomed into. An accident, an illness and the everyday natural effects of aging can affect anyone. This is why having a robust theology of disability informed by lived experience can benefit the whole Church in general and why good access can have secondary benefits for the whole family of God.

Proclaim justice

I am often struck by the fact that the first public ministry Jesus undertook involved preaching a message of liberation for oppressed bodies. After Jesus' own wilderness experience, he enters the synagogue and preaches from the prophet Isaiah:

> The Spirit of the Lord is upon me,
> because he has anointed me
> to bring good news to the poor.
> He has sent me to proclaim release to the captives
> and recovery of sight to the blind,
> to let the oppressed go free,
> to proclaim the year of the Lord's favour.
> (Luke 4:18-19)

Here is Jesus' mission statement: To proclaim release, recovery and freedom. To offer good news. Disabled people long to hear that good news proclaimed from those in power in our pulpits. And they long to be enabled and empowered to share that good news themselves, both to their own communities and to the Church at large.

Jesus told a story in Luke 14 about those invited to his banquet. When guests were initially invited many made excuses or had better offers. Jesus then says that the master instructed his servant to 'Go out at once into the streets and lanes of the town and bring in the poor, the crippled, the blind, and the lame.' Jesus sets out a vision where those on the margins are sought out and brought into the banquet. The table is open and accessible to all who accept. There are no access restraints to the table of God. We are longing for the Church to live that out as a reality today and not just a hope for eternity.

Disability justice activist Mia Mingus describes disability solidarity like this: 'I want to be with you.

If you can't go, then I don't want to go.'[10] Here we have an echo of Ruth's promise to Naomi in the Hebrew scriptures. How could we live out this kind of disability solidarity in churches? If you can't get to the raised altar, I will not receive communion there either. If you experience sensory overload because of the lights and noise in church, I will worship outside the gates with you. Disabled people in the CofE are calling out for justice. Inclusion is an admirable target for churches and, yes, we are calling to be included in the life of the Church; but far too often inclusion can be a call to *assimilation*. A call for disabled people to fit themselves into the existing, often ableist, structures rather than an attempt to address the structures themselves and, where needed, to dismantle and rebuild them.

It is our hope and prayer that Archbishop Sarah will help disabled members of the Church of England in this work of dismantling and rebuilding through advocacy and enabling our ministries. Together we can work towards building a Church where all bodies and minds are able to flourish and take their valued place within the all-encompassing Body of Christ.

[1] https://nobodyisdisposable.org/about/
[2] This conference has been running since 2012, run by disabled people for disabled people and aims to resource one another and the Church.
[3] https://www.scope.org.uk/media/disability-facts-figures
[4] https://www.trussell.org.uk/our-work/ending-the-need-for-food-banks/equity-diversity-and-inclusion
[5] Nancy L. Eisland unpacked this way of speaking about God in her book of the same name, *The Disabled God: Toward a Liberatory Theology of Disability*, published by ABNDP - Abingdon Press, 1994
[6] *From Disability: The Inclusive Church Resource*, published by Darton, Longman and Todd, 2014
[7] https://www.churchofengland.org/resources/barrier-free-

[8] belonging/disability-project-2024-26
[8] Quoted on a recent Diocese of London Disability Ministry podcast, Sep 2025
[9] https://www.churchofengland.org/media/press-releases/assisted-suicide-law-would-make-country-says-some-lives-are-not-worth-living-bishop-london
[10] https://leavingevidence.wordpress.com/2010/05/03/where-ever-you-are-is-where-i-want-to-be-crip-solidarity/

PRAYER

Liberating God,

Help us to work towards a Church where all bodies and minds are welcomed and celebrated. May we follow the example of Jesus who welcomed all to his accessible table, treating those he met with compassion and dignity as fearfully and wonderfully made children of God.

Grant us the courage to confront systems that exclude and help us dismantle barriers built by fear, misunderstanding, and indifference.

Teach us the value of interdependence: to recognise that our flourishing is bound together. May we learn that a Church without disabled people is a disabled Church and honour disabled members of the Church of England not as flaws to be fixed but as gifts carrying wisdom, creativity, and truth.

Strengthen Archbishop Sarah and all who lead your Church. Help us to listen deeply to disabled and neurodiverse voices and allow them to transform our culture, inform our decisions and shape our future as we seek a Church of justice for all.

Amen.

4
Sitting Outside, Encountering Christ

The Church of England, LGBTQIA Inclusion and Same-Sex Marriage

Charlie Baczyk-Bell

> For some, the simple fact that I have led this process has meant that they see me as no longer in communion with them. I want to assure them that I still believe that we are in communion with one another. And whilst I may no longer be invited to eat at their table, they will always be welcome at mine. And if that means that I need to sit outside with the powerless, the marginalized, the lost, then that's where I will sit. And I am certain that I will also encounter Christ there. To see the other made in the image of God, allows us to see them not as the other, but with equity, as God sees them, with the love which Jesus Christ sees the other.

So spoke the then Bishop of London in November 2023, as she closed yet another fractious debate on the Living in Love and Faith (LLF) process, ostensibly set up to enable 'radical new Christian inclusion' for LGBTQIA people. The process has been a deep disappointment – made more disappointing by the hopes that were raised when, in February 2023, it appeared the Church might, finally, have something positive to say about LGBTQIA people, being cruelly dashed. Heading up the process at that stage was Bishop Sarah – someone whose views were not entirely known, but who was a trusted and serious member of the House of Bishops with a reputation – fairly gained – for getting things done, for being no-nonsense, and for being pastoral.

By the time that now Archbishop Sarah Mullally is installed in Canterbury Cathedral, it appears that there is an intention to 'draw a line' under LLF as a process, not least because it has failed. Bishop Sarah has not been at the head of it for some time, and it's fair to suggest that things have seriously derailed since she was. The Church of England has gotten itself caught up in endless, fruitless, debates about new 'structures' – which self-professed conservatives have claimed that they 'need' for the most meagre change of pastoral provision for LGBTQIA people. We have gotten to a place where, yet again, LGBTQIA people have found themselves sacrificed on the altar of 'unity' (itself a vague and somewhat confused concept) – the apology of 2023 fading into the far distance, and the harm (spiritual and otherwise) is immense.

It didn't need to end this way – and it ought not to have done so. The reasons for it happening are multifarious. It is without doubt the case that lack of episcopal strategy, archiepiscopal interference, carefully manipulated central control by unelected officials, threats of withdrawal of money and promises of pseudo-ordinations and schismatic behaviour – all played their part. At root, it failed because its aim collided with a refusal by people refusing to contemplate any meaningful change, however modest, or any willingness to live together across difference. Various groups have been determined to hold the Church to ransom during the process – refusing to compromise, and casting people like Bishop Sarah, whose record shows that she is in favour of change, as somehow unorthodox, as failing to uphold her ordination vows, as having 'repeatedly promoted unbiblical and revisionist teachings regarding marriage and sexual morality'.[1] Opposition has come from within and outside the Church of England – most of it smelling more than a little of misogyny, however much pain is taken to make clear that it's Bishop Sarah's 'views' and not her being a woman that is the issue.

It is certainly true that Archbishop Sarah has not been a visible campaigner on LGBTQIA affirmation by the Church of England. She was not, for example, one of the forty-four who called for the Church to get on with it back in November 2023, but then again that may well have been because she was running the LLF project and she was seeking to be fair.[2] Yet many who have spoken with her individually, and certainly my own experience of her, is that she is pastoral and sensitive, wishes the Church to find a way to meet the pastoral needs of LGBTQIA people, and to stop casting them as 'the other'. She wants change. I think, too, that she understands intersectionality – that the abuse that women clergy continue to receive from some quarters (including both macro- and micro-aggressions) is all part-and-parcel of a wider oppressive landscape that continues to blight the Church of England's polity, which imagines the straight, white, cis-gendered, heterosexual, non-disabled, middle-class male as being the normative against which everything else is compared, unfavourably.

Herein, then, I think lies our first caution when it comes to what we might hope for or expect from Archbishop Sarah's archiepiscopate. Many people, from around the communion, have asked me how her appointment is going to affect LGBTQIA people. My response is clear – let us not overburden her with unreasonable expectations. The Archbishop of Canterbury is not a Chief Executive Officer, nor an Anglican Pope, however much her predecessors might have suggested this is the case! The archbishop is primarily a diocesan bishop and a chief pastor – everything else comes after that (of which more below). She won't have executive power over a cabinet of bishops – that is simply not how our ecclesiology works. There will doubtless be people hoping she falls, and indeed attempting to contribute to that becoming the case. It is certainly true that the archbishop sets the tone – for good and for ill – and it is also true that endless and often unhelpful interference or flip-flopping, or overly controlling managerialism, from some previous archbishops has done a lot of damage. Yet we ought to be very wary of those who will immediately seek to blame her for whatever they don't like about the Church of England. It's unjust, and unfair, and untrue, and we ought to be better than that.

All that said, I did meet the appointment of Bishop Sarah to Canterbury with a sense of hope for LGBTQIA people, for several reasons. As I've noted already, she is someone who gets things done, who is pastoral and kind, and who understands the intersectional nature of the struggle. She is also someone who appears to grasp that this is not primarily a matter of managing different groups of people, or indeed a matter of false unity creation, but rather a matter of justice. LGBTQIA people ought to be included in the life of the Church not because it will shut us up, or because of some vague secular 'woke' social justice lens. LGBTQIA people ought to be recognised as full members of the Body of Christ because not to do so lessens that Body – it is a blasphemy, a violence done to the Church that Christ founded. LGBTQIA people are an essential part of the Body, and until that is recognised, not only with warm words, but with actions that not only seek to include but to learn from LGBTQIA people, then we fail to live up to being the Church we are called to be. We are less than we can be, and so our ability to live out the Gospel is diminished. LGBTQIA affirmation is not an optional add-on to the 'real' Gospel – it is inextricably linked to the very message of salvation, to the good news for all people that the Son of God was sent to bring.

I write this chapter having just celebrated the first Vespers of Advent in Bethlehem, as part of a General Synod solidarity trip to the Holy Land. The people of Palestine are suffering to a degree which we in comfortable England cannot begin to imagine. They suffer through our silence, and they suffer through our inaction. They cry out for justice, and we appear to be deaf to those cries. They suffer in the land where Jesus was incarnated – made fully human, fleshly, just like us, yet without sin.

The incarnation, it seems to me, is a hugely underappreciated part of our faith, and our failure to speak of it, and of the place of Christ's birth (and all the horrors meted out on this place), is deeply damaging. We talk endlessly about the crucifixion and the resurrection – entirely understandably. Yet in our desire to talk about the end of Jesus' life, we often seem to forget to talk about the start, and about the implications of Jesus being a human being, walking the ground upon which we walk, being flesh and blood with all that entails. Jesus the God is easier for us to imagine sometimes than Jesus the human.

This has shown itself to be true in debates around sexuality and gender in the Church of England in huge measure. Far too often, we have shown our deep squeamishness about the idea that we might be embodied humans – preferring to talk in the abstract, which is all rather less icky than the reality. We do this when we talk about 'the gay issue' rather than talking about LGBTQIA people – and we do it when we refuse to define what it is that some LGTBQIA people are supposed not to be doing when we demand they remain celibate. Bishops and synods laugh when asked whether they would like to define what sexual intimacy is for LGBTQIA people, yet still they continue to try to ban it – an absurdity, if it were not so cruel. The mere mention of genitals or body parts in the General Synod leads to blushes and clutched pearls, and LGBTQIA people, who are often denied even the basics of human dignity, are told to 'just wait a little longer', while straights go home to their husbands and wives.

Yet pretending and lying has become the official *modus operandum* of the Church of England when it comes to matters of the body, including sexuality and gender. Our record on safeguarding is atrocious, and that is not separable from our unwillingness to get real about sexual propriety, about bodies, consent, and human dignity. A Church that cannot speak truthfully about bodies will never be able to safeguard the vulnerable nor to proclaim the embodied God of the Incarnation. For years, our moral positioning on sexual morality has related entirely to 'homophiles' – an unfortunate term, cemented into the life of the Church of England through the (entirely unwarranted and inexplicable) deification of the document *Issues in Human Sexuality*, implemented when I was barely born and only extricated from our processes in 2025 thanks to the courage of Mae Christie, a priest from the Diocese of Southwark.[3] Questions about sexual propriety were almost exclusively posed to those who *appeared* to be LGBTQIA as a result of this pernicious and vicious little document, and ordinands were encouraged to either lie or to commit themselves to a celibacy that was anything but freely chosen, poorly defined, and very likely to either destroy relationships or fail.

Yet whilst the detested *Issues* is gone, life has not suddenly become better for LGBTQIA people in the life of the Church of England. Still, we are not allowed to offer 'standalone' services of blessing – although, of course, 'allowed' is doing a lot of heavy lifting there, and in my view and that of several canon lawyers, priests are entirely entitled to offer them under the provision of the canons. Priests are *still* not permitted to get married to someone of the same sex or gender, and such a marriage remains an absolute impediment to ordination. Everyone knows that this is unjust – yet here we are, with no change after years of debate and discussion. This is the Church that Archbishop Sarah is inheriting, and it is not a happy place.

So a hope that I have for the new archbishop is that she recalls the Church to remember that Jesus Christ was incarnated before He was crucified – that he needed a body, a real human body, to be crucified and raised, and that this body bore the marks of the nails and the spear when He appeared in the Upper Room. Archbishop Sarah has spoken movingly of her time as a nurse, of her washing of feet that 'has shaped my Christian vocation as a nurse, then a priest, then a bishop. In the apparent chaos which surrounds us, in the midst of such profound global uncertainty, the possibility of healing lies in acts of kindness and love.'[4] Of course, it is very much in line with Bishop Sarah's lack of showiness that she rarely mentions that not only was she a nurse, but a very senior NHS leader before she was forty, but it is also a sign that in her ministry as nurse as in her ministry as bishop, the fundamentals remain key.

Washing of feet may appear to be mere ritual, but for someone who has worked as a nurse, this can never be the case – and I say this as a doctor who is endlessly in awe of the dedication and sheer humanity of my nursing colleagues, who often put us to shame. I would suggest that foot washing as ritual and foot washing as embodied reality cannot be neatly separated in someone with these two vocations. It is a sign of humility, and it is a sign of incarnation – a sign that the Church is called not to ignore the messiness of human life, but to embrace it, and to name it, and to bend down and wash and kiss the feet that tread the pilgrim road.

It is a sign, too, of justice. 'The possibility of healing lies in acts of kindness and love' says our new archbishop, when talking about washing feet, and kindness and love require, and conversely lead to, a call to and for justice. Justice is in the very heart of God, and justice is part of the holiness of God that we are each called to embody and live into in our vocation to Christian ministry, whatever that ministry will be. Allowing a lack of justice – whether that is unjust structures, or unjust societies, or unjust measures, or merely acts of injustice – to go unchallenged is to turn our face away from Christ. Allowing injustice to prevail for one moment longer when we have the opportunity to combat it and change course is to fail in our basic vocation to follow Christ.

The reality is that the Church of England, and its bishops, have failed in that vocation time and again when they have allowed the cries of the vulnerable and the oppressed to be ignored. Amongst the most visible of those oppressed – of those 'othered' by powerful forces within the Church, the 'acceptable sacrifice' – are LGBTQIA people. Repeatedly, we have been told that it's just too hard, that our dignity is not worth the effort. We're not the first people to be treated like this, and we won't be the last. However, we are the people currently facing this right now in the Church, and it is incumbent upon the next Archbishop of Canterbury to play her part in bringing about the much overdue change. I think Bishop Sarah understands that we cannot go on like this. I hope that she sees it as more of a priority than keeping the peace or pleasing those who will never be pleased.

Of course, the current playing field is anything but easy. Along with Neil Patterson, Helen King, Nic Tall, and a group of others, we founded Together for the Church of England a few years ago, to give the progressive mainstream a better co-ordinated voice in the structures of the Church of England. I don't imagine any archbishop really enjoys General Synod, but it's an unfortunate fact of life in the current Church and represents a (frankly rather unrepresentative) hurdle for any change to be brought about. Indeed, Archbishop Justin Welby, towards the end of his archiepiscopate, made clear to progressives that we needed to organise better – and organise better we have. In the first year of her archiepiscopate, Archbishop Sarah will have a new Synod, with what we must hope will be a more representative and progressive majority. This is a majority who wishes her well, and which wants her to succeed. It is a majority who sees justice issues as part of the very fabric of the Gospel, and it is a majority which will not rest until LGBTQIA people are fully embraced as fellow disciples on the road. There is hope and possibility for her as she walks into the role, and a real sense of purpose.

Yet, all that being said, this does not take away from the fact that there will remain forces at play which will seek to undermine or question Archbishop Sarah's authority. I have already mentioned the GAFCON statement, yet there will be elements within our own Church, too, desperate for her to fail.

For far too long, the Anglican Communion has been used as a convenient foil for so-called conservatives in the Church of England, who are too lily-livered to admit that they don't want any more dignity to be granted for LGBTQIA people and would rather blame it on 'the communion'. Lazy stereotyping abounds, and people from the 'Global South' are instrumentalised and used as pawns in a game of money and power that all too often finds its genesis within the 'Global North'. Over the past ten years, the Anglican Communion has shown increasing signs of tension and, indeed, has begun to fragment, yet precious little proper analysis has been given to the underlying colonial dynamics. The role of Archbishop as an English diocesan and as the 'spiritual leader' of the communion is broken. Neither of Bishop Sarah's predecessors were willing to say that. I hope that she has the strength of character to do so.

For if she doesn't, then it is hard to see how LGBTQIA people can be anything more than a political football in a colonial Anglican Communion. This may well require a fundamental rethinking of the Communion and its structures, but if the alternative is that LGBTQIA people, both in England and across the Communion, are to be silenced and told to suffer for the benefit of the whole, then it is well beyond time (to say nothing of the need to decolonise and to recognise the postcolonial nature of the Communion in any case). A revitalised Communion founded on fellowship and friendship, which is not driven by questions of money, control, and power, is a much healthier form of *koinonia*. Indeed, to return to the cries for justice in Palestine, and in so many other parts of our broken world, if the Archbishop of Canterbury might be able to speak as an equal amongst equals, making present the voices of the vulnerable around the Communion in the corridors of power, then we might get a little closer to what we might become. Imagine what that might be like – that the Archbishop of Canterbury might speak from the margins where *'the powerless, the marginalized, the lost'* are found. Where she might again proclaim that she wishes us all *'to see the other made in the image of God'*. How this might allow *'us to see them not as the other, but with equity, as God sees them, with the love which Jesus Christ sees the other'*. The Anglican Communion does not need to be a zero-sum game. There are serious things to talk about and even to agree about that don't relate to same-sex relationships. It is up to the new Archbishop to make that plain, and to refuse to be trapped in an endless circular conversation about sex. Get back to mercy and compassion for the vulnerable. *'And whilst I may no longer be invited to eat at their table, they will always be welcome at mine'* seems as theological a statement on *koinonia* as there might ever be.

So, whilst the situation is anything but easy for the new archbishop, nonetheless there is a future of genuinely hopeful possibility – but this future will require courage, and solidarity, and support. It goes without saying that we need to move swiftly to correct the injustices of today – as far as LGBTQIA affirmation goes, at the very least, promptly moving to services of blessing and enabling clergy to hold a cure and be married to someone of the same sex. In the short term, too, we need to have the debate on same-sex marriage, and Archbishop Sarah should have the courage of her convictions and speak clearly and plainly. For far too long, being an episcopal 'focus of unity' (and particularly an archiepiscopal focus of unity[5]) has meant saying nothing, doing very little, hoping things will go away, or at the very least hoping that hand-wringing will be enough to keep LGBTQIA people in the tent. This simply won't do any more.

In other words, if the Church of England is to be serious about LGBTQIA inclusion, then it needs to embrace same-sex marriage as a bare minimum and move towards a position where it really seeks to learn from and alongside queer Christians. It needs to recognise that it *needs* us in the Body of Christ to truly *be* the Body of Christ. Queer people have a huge amount to offer to the Church (indeed, have already offered so much) and they have the right to do so with dignity and holiness. Queer people, indeed, need to be enabled to flourish, to serve without fear, to be received as gifts to the Body of Christ. The new archbishop will set the tone of the conversation as we move forwards, and I hope and pray she will have the courage to do so in a way that is unambiguously welcoming, true, and pastoral.

It won't be easy, and there will be bumps along the way – but bumps are so much easier to bear when we know that our spiritual leader actually loves us like her children, like Jesus does. Yes, there will need to be compromises, some of which will be painful – but none of which can be allowed to deny the dignity of the children of God. LGBTQIA affirmation is not a pastoral concession or an optional extra, but a matter of Christian justice and fidelity to the incarnation. Queer people are sick to the back teeth of being treated as second class citizens, and the new Archbishop herself knows how that can feel in a Church that still refuses to give full dignity to its ordained women. She comes into the role in a time of anxiety and fear, but a time that can be transformed through hope lived courageously, faithfully, and lovingly. She does so with our abundant prayers – may she continue to encounter Christ at the excluded tables, and may we be there alongside her in solidarity.

1. GAFCON, 'Communique: Canterbury Appointment Abandons Anglicans', https://gafcon.org/communique-updates/canterbury-appointment-abandons-anglicans/ [accessed 29th November 2025].
2. Thinking Anglicans, '44 bishops call for clergy to be allowed same-sex civil marriages', https://www.thinkinganglicans.org.uk/44-bishops-call-for-clergy-to-be-allowed-same-sex-civil-marriages/ [accessed 29th November 2025].
3. In what is called a Private Members Motion – that is, in a process that was not led by the House of Bishops, highlighting once again their inability to lead on matters of inclusion.
4. Address by The Rt Revd and Rt Hon Dame Sarah Mullally, https://www.archbishopofcanterbury.org/news/news-and-statements/address-rt-revd-and-rt-hon-dame-sarah-mullally [accessed 29th November 2025].
5. For example in Archbishop Justin Welby's mystifying decision to rejoice over but not offer Prayers of Love and Faith, as described in BBC News, 'Archbishop will not give new blessing for gay couples', https://www.bbc.co.uk/news/uk-64342940 [accessed 29th November 2025].

PRAYER

Lord God, you have called your servant Sarah to be pastor to your people
And you call us all to form the Body of Christ.
Renew your Church,
And bless Sarah with the gifts of compassion, mercy, and truth.
Pour out your abundant blessing on her as she seeks to follow you,
Guide her along dark paths,
Bless her abundantly,
Anoint her with the oil of gladness.
Whisper words of hope to her in times of tumult,
Protect her in the time of trial,
And lead her to holy encounter with the excluded.
Grant her the wisdom, audacity, and faith
To dare to lead us closer to your reign.
The Kingdom of Heaven has come near, good news for all people:
Amen, let it be true, Lord Christ.

5
When Rights are Rolled Back, 'Let Justice Roll Like a River'

Trans and Non-Binary People and the Church of England

Christina Beardsley SMMS

'And Sarah laughed'

In response to God's seemingly impossible promise that she would bear a child in old age, Sarah laughed. Did you laugh, I wonder, when you heard that you had been appointed Archbishop of Canterbury?

Laughter seems a healthy response to the prospect of assuming what is a daunting, and increasingly impossible, role – a visceral sign of trust in God alone. God has called you and will provide the means to do it.

I can picture that scene, as you are such a smiley bishop – how we'll miss your smile in the Diocese of London. Formerly a stern-faced cardinal, Jose Bergoglio emerged on the balcony after his election as a smiley pope. In prayer, prior to greeting the city and the world for the first time, something shifted within him: God touched him. May you too share this blessing, a similar lightness of spirit amidst great responsibilities. There will be tears (more on this later) and trials aplenty ahead. May they never diminish the joy of knowing that you, and God's people, are in God's care.

First among equals

On becoming archbishop, you will be a primate, the Primate of All England. Though the Archbishop of Canterbury is not – as we're often reminded – an Anglican Pope. Among the Primates of the Anglican Communion, and within the Church of England's House of Bishops, you will be 'primus inter pares', first among equals.

What a beautiful phrase that is: 'first among equals'. For you share this equality with all baptised people, indeed with all people, made in the image of God.

In this chapter I'm inviting you to consider how, in your new role, you might be able to improve the lives of a specific group: gender diverse people – those who are trans or non-binary.

I'm sure you'll have noticed that the rights of gender diverse people are being steadily eroded in this country. It started, coincidentally, in 2018, a year after the Church of England's Living in Love and Faith (LLF) project was launched.

LLF looked at identity, sexuality, relationships, and marriage, but while trans people, including myself, were involved, our lives weren't central to it. LLF's main outcomes – though progress has halted even here – were the Prayers of Love and Faith (PLF) for use with same sex couples, and whether ordinands and clergy may enter a same sex civil marriage. In fact, these things *do* matter for some trans and non-binary people (I'll say more later) – despite claims that they only affect people who are LGB, and not those who are T.

Important as marriage and relationships are for UK gender diverse people, our greatest concern now is the threat to our civil rights that has been gathering pace in the past seven years. For a brief decade and a half, following the passing of the Gender Recognition Act 2004, trans people began to shed shame and stigma. Greater visibility led to social acceptance, but all this was reversed, almost overnight, by a relentless, and well-financed, demonising of trans people by the UK press, media, and some politicians. The UK's trans population is roughly equivalent to that of its Jewish population. Imagine the outcry had the UK media turned on any other minority in this way.

International experts have described what is happening as verging on genocide. Currently there are no openly trans MPs, or members of the House of Lords. The UK's most senior trans judge retired early due to the transphobia she experienced and relocated to Ireland. Trans people are routinely discussed in the media, but unlikely to participate in the conversation in the current toxic climate.

No longer seen as equal as human beings, I am looking to you, Sarah, as a spiritual leader, and first among equals, to advocate for us in our Church and country. Your National Health Service background, commitment to pastoral ministry, and familiarity with the corridors of power, makes you ideally equipped to help us.

What follows are some ways in which you could use your new authority on behalf of gender diverse people.

The Supreme Court?

I'm increasingly convinced by historians who regard the introduction of the UK Supreme Court as an unwelcome innovation, disruptive to Britain's system of government. Hitherto, in the United Kingdom, Parliament was 'the supreme court'. Now parliamentary sovereignty is compromised by a semi-autonomous panel of judges able to overrule the country's elected government. This development has been especially devastating for UK trans people.

Spy Wednesday

On 16 April 2025, the UK Supreme Court ruled, in the case For Women Scotland versus The Scottish Ministers, that 'sex' in the Equality Act refers to biological sex at birth. The Court arrived at this Judgment having relied heavily on anti-trans arguments from the For Women Scotland's legal team. Trans people and experts in equality law relating to gender diverse people were excluded from the process.

Publication of the Judgment was met with shock and astonishment, but worse was to come. The news broke in the middle of Holy Week, sometimes called Spy Wednesday, recalling the day Judas Iscariot resolved to hand Jesus to the authorities and ensnare him. A day associated with Christ's betrayal seemed apt for this announcement, as many UK trans people have felt betrayed by the Supreme Court Judgment.

I began to receive text messages from cisgender clergy friends troubled by the Court's decision and worried on my behalf. Although touched by their care, I thought they were over-reacting. This was a technical matter, surely, with little practical consequence. Our institutions could be trusted to protect us.

My friends were proved right, though, and my naïve trust in human reasonableness was further shattered, when another semi-autonomous body, the Equality and Human Rights Commission (EHRC), misapplied the Judgment by issuing interim guidance that sought to exclude trans people from public spaces. That development was still to come, but my cisgender friends foresaw it better than I could.

Maundy Thursday

At the Maundy Thursday Chrism Mass in St Paul's Cathedral, at which you presided and preached, Sarah, one of these friends, on her way to receive Holy Communion, left the queue, made her way towards me, and flung her arms around me. That embrace, in that place, and on such a holy day – the day Jesus commanded us to love one another as He has loved us – was the safest setting for me to start to accept that our lives as trans people were now under threat: from the State itself.

After Mass, over coffee in the Crypt, my friend made a beeline for you, as our bishop, to share her concerns, and like a good shepherd you sought and found me. When we talked, you spoke about other trans clergy we knew, and the Judgment's implications, depending on people's circumstances. I was still in denial then, but not anymore.

The role of Parliament

Since then, it's emerged that people hostile to trans people were purposely appointed to the EHRC, and that the anti-trans organisation, Sex Matters, had privileged access and input to the Commission's deliberations, while trans organisations were conspicuously ignored. Following a 'consultation', whose results the Commission has tried to hide, a revised Code of Practice was sent to the Women and Equalities Minister, and could become statutory guidance without parliamentary scrutiny.

Given this blatant assault on trans people's rights, there's increasing pressure for Parliament to review the EHRC's proposals. Many suspect they will prove unworkable. The interim guidance has already harmed gender non-conforming cisgender women in public spaces, and created a climate of fear among Britain's trans population. A recent YouGov poll revealed that eighty-four per cent of the UK trans people surveyed experienced Britain as unsafe.

Were the EHRC's Code of Practice to receive cross-party scrutiny and debate in Parliament, I urge you to lead the Lords Spiritual in defending trans people's right to privacy, and continued access to gendered public spaces, like toilets and hospital wards, that match their gender identity and expression. Being first among equals gives you the authority to lead on this, as in other areas.

One heart and mind

I realise that the House of Bishops is not of one mind about trans people. The LLF book acknowledged that, but even bishops with theological reservations about gender transition, must be troubled by the increasing stigma and unethical treatment UK trans people are experiencing. Trans people's rights, including medical treatment, are being undermined or withdrawn, by institutional infiltration, manipulation of evidence and false claims.

For example, existing legislation already includes provision to exclude a trans person from a single sex space for a justifiable reason. Or again, the belief that trans women are a threat to other women is demonstrably false. Statistically, trans women are far more vulnerable to verbal and physical abuse in public spaces, while violence against women and girls is perpetrated mainly by cisgender males.

You have spoken courageously in the Lord's debates on assisted dying. Please speak up for trans people when our lives are discussed in the High Court of Parliament, and encourage the other Lords Spiritual to do the same.

If the bishops are split, intellectually, about trans people's experience, they must surely be undivided – of one heart – about the worth of every person made in the image of God. From being treated (almost) as equals under the law, trans people risk being seen as less than human. It's time to speak out – from the heart.

The tears of things

I've mentioned Sarah's laughter. There's a tradition that Sarah wept (when Abraham took Isaac to Mount Moriah). Life is full of tears, and you are not afraid to weep in public. You shed tears at General Synod, speaking about the micro-aggressions you'd experienced as a woman in ministry. Presumably there have been macro-aggressions as well, for the same reason, with more to come following your appointment as archbishop.

A pioneer, you've broken through the stained-glass ceiling, but as a woman, you won't be considered an equal by everyone. For some you will be 'equal but different', an office holder in the Church, but not really a priest, let alone a bishop. How similar that sounds to trans people's experience!

Even when our gender is recognised by law, we're accused of perpetrating a 'legal fiction', and not being who we say we are, an 'office holder', rather than the real thing. It seems that trans people experience aggressions – micro and macro – not unlike those directed at women clergy!

Add to this that gender equality remains a dream for many women. It's enough to make one weep – and to press for change (we'll come to that) – but there's more.

Not for turning

Turning is expected of Christians. In the gospel Jesus calls us to repent, to turn around from our own preoccupations, and walk with Him into the kingdom of God. We humans must change our ways, in response to God's love, which is gloriously unchanging: steadfast, reliable, and generous too. It's sad then that the Church of England can often seem grudging and conditional. Sad too that, having repented of past failings, it so easily forgets what has been agreed, revisiting and even overturning earlier decisions.

In July 2017, when General Synod passed the Blackburn motion to welcome and affirm trans people, the subsequent statement was unequivocal. 'The Church of England welcomes and encourages the unconditional affirmation of trans people, equally with all people, within the body of Christ, and rejoices in the diversity of that body into which all Christians have been baptized by one Spirit.'

A recent Church of England communique, following the Supreme Court Judgment, however, includes the notion of competing rights, apparently forgetful of our Church's – uncompromising and theologically grounded – position on trans people. Like the society in which it is set, the Church seems to be rowing back, as has happened with the Prayers of Love and Faith. With you at the helm as archbishop, I hope the Church will have the courage and integrity to uphold synodical decisions, and resist the pressure to overturn what the majority has agreed.

Young ones
You and I have both worked in the health service (in the same hospital, though at different times), you at the most senior level. Are you disturbed, as I am, by the withdrawal of trans affirming care for young people?

A concerted campaign led to the subsequent closure of the Tavistock Clinic, noted for its cautious approach, but falsely accused of rushing young people into transition. New regional clinics were promised to replace it, but these have been delayed, partly due to disagreements over the benefits of gender affirming care – an option that hardly exists any more in the NHS for children and adolescents.

Clinical pathways for gender diverse young people have been road-blocked, and their lives devastated, by this extraordinary turn around, in defiance of best practice in other Western countries. Key here is the ban on puberty blockers for gender diverse young people, but not for those with precocious puberty, for whom they continue to be prescribed. The targeting of trans youngsters could hardly be clearer.

The Health Minister, Wes Streeting, has justified the ban citing the Cass report, a document widely discredited by specialists in the field. A paediatrician, though with no expertise in this area, Dr Hilary Cass and her team have been criticised for research bias. Put simply, the Cass report advocates a cautious approach – the reality anyway, given treatment was hard to access – and revives or implies the dangerous notion, overturned by the World Health Organisation, that gender variance is a mental illness, rather than a naturally occurring human variation.

Some of the young people affected have already fought back, occupying the Department of Health after the Health Secretary refused to meet with them, and staging 'die ins' in public spaces to highlight the suicides that have followed the withdrawal of life-giving care. It seems they can stick up for themselves, but I'd love to hear you debate on their behalf with Dr Cass, now a baroness, in the House of Lords. Maybe you could have a word with her in the tearoom. I've met her and she seems an affable person, but she needs to understand the harm she has done.

Conversion therapy

Conversion is an arresting word to describe our turning to Christ, from whom, as the song says, there should be 'no turning back'. Conversion therapy, so called, is not well-named. We can turn from our sinful ways to renew our walk with Christ, but what we can't do is change fundamental aspects of our human nature. The UK's therapeutic bodies are unanimous that it is both ineffective and potentially harmful to attempt to change a person's sexual orientation or gender identity. Yet the withdrawal of affirming care for gender diverse children and adolescents does precisely that. For almost a decade, successive UK governments have promised a comprehensive ban on conversion therapy. Such are the toxic attitudes to trans people, that we are identified as probably being the cause of this delay, with some arguing that we are confused lesbian and gay people, and gender transition itself a form of conversion therapy. Some people seem ready to believe anything about us, except what we ourselves have to say!

When the Bill to ban these practices comes before Parliament, I hope it will be trans inclusive, as promised, and that you and the other Lords Spiritual will be willing to support it. Much of the opposition is coming from conservative religious voices, including a member of the Archbishops Council. I'd happily see you turn back the clock and abolish that body, introduced by one of your predecessors, George Carey, as if the Church of England didn't have enough bureaucratic layers.

An agreed definition of homophobia, biphobia and transphobia would help. The Church of England Schools anti-bullying guidance, *Valuing All God's Children*, would be a useful starting point. Other denominations have tighter clergy codes of conduct in relation to LGBTQ+ people from which we could also learn.

Leadership

What I'm hoping for, once you've assumed the Chair of St Augustine, is leadership from you and the bishops. We're frequently told that the Church of England is episcopally led and synodically governed, but despite being a buzz word in recent decades, leadership has been seriously lacking, especially in relation to gender and sexuality, with our concerns lost in committee, or obfuscated behind the language of law.

Presumably this is because the bishops have been divided on same-sex marriage and trans people. PCCs are often divided about things, so is Parliament, as are local councils, but they make decisions, nevertheless.

Issues in human sexuality is an example. For years this document was misused in the discernment process for ordination. Most people knew this to be wrong and the bishops could have withdrawn it at any point, but they didn't. It took a private members motion to remove it. The leadership was lacking.

Postcode Lottery

Differences among the bishops are both inevitable and an enrichment, but harmful when they conflict with the Church of England's stated position. There are dioceses where trans clergy would not be unconditionally affirmed or employable given the bishop's views.

Marriage à-la-mode

Trans people are also affected by the Church of England's unwillingness to accommodate same-sex marriage and the complexity of their relationships, like those individuals who have married as the gender with which they identify but without legal gender recognition, and who may not be legally married. Or clergy and laity in an opposite sex marriage who transition and are then told that they are in a same-sex marriage. Or non-binary people, whose legal status isn't recognised in the UK, but who seek God's blessing on their relationships just like other people. LLF began to engage with these realities, but the Church of England seems to be in flight from lived experience now.

Sarah too is among the prophets

The matters I've raised involve leadership – and more: prophetic ministry.

Most well-known biblical prophets are men, but seven women are also considered prophets, Sarah being one.

Might you Sarah, soon to be at the heart of the British Establishment, become a prophet for those on our country's margins – the poor, the migrant, the disabled, and, at this crucial time, the trans community? That's my hope and my prayer.

PRAYER

God of the margins,
you sent your Son
to welcome home those on the edges of their
    communities,
pour your Holy Spirit on your daughter Sarah,
to equip her with prophetic edginess
on behalf of
trans and non-binary people:
may she speak for the silenced or ignored,
challenge falsehoods about their lives,
and be their advocate when rights are overturned,
or their dignity as your children
is questioned, threatened, or betrayed.
We ask this in the name of Jesus Christ,
who with you and the Holy Spirit
are perfect love, unconquerable and undying,
now, and forever.
Amen.

6
Falling Among Thieves: Understanding and Responding to Church-Related Abuse

Abuse, Safeguarding and the Church of England

Andrew Graystone

For more than a decade, the life of the Church of England has been dominated by the painful unfolding of stories of abuse within its own ranks. Those who have been wounded by high profile Christian leaders such as Bishop Peter Ball, Bishop Victor Whitsey, Canon Mike Pilavachi, and John Smyth QC join countless other victims in reciting a litany of pain and shame. The Church's response has been, and continues to be, managerial, chaotic and ineffective. Central spending on safeguarding in the Church of England has risen from around £50,000 per annum when Justin Welby was made archbishop in 2013 to well over £7 million just ten years later. Yet in spite of countless new posts, debates in the General Synod, vigils, and endless committees and initiatives, and in spite of repeated insistence that 'victims must come first', the Church doesn't seem able to grip the issue in a meaningful or effective way.

The strange truth is that after all this time, many leaders in the Church can't effectively articulate what abuse *is*, nor do they know what it would mean to respond to it in a Christian way. In the absence of this understanding, the Church treats abuse as a civil wrong rather than a spiritual one, offering only secular answers to profoundly religious questions perhaps out of fear that if it were to be treated as a spiritual issue, the questions that followed would be too searching. Managerialism and delay fill the gap, and victims of abuse complain that this response re-abuses them. One of the drawbacks of this way of thinking is that it sees abuse as an event, in which the emphasis is on the actions of the abuser, rather than the impact on the victim. Almost no victims of church-related abuse report that they have been helped or satisfied by the Church's response. Many say that they regret ever having disclosed their abuse to the Church. Many church leaders are exhausted and frustrated by this issue too, some to the point of giving up.

The mandatory safeguarding training that happens in every parish focuses on how to spot the signs of abuse, and when and where to report it. Rarely does someone ask, 'Where is the power in this church, this diocese, this meeting - and how is it being wielded?'

Archbishop Sarah understands this. Speaking on her appointment as Archbishop-designate on 3 October 2025, she said, 'As a Church we have too often failed to recognise or take seriously the misuse of power in all its forms. Our history of safeguarding failures have left a legacy of deep harm and mistrust, and we must all be willing to have light shone on our actions, regardless of our role in the Church.' Now she assumes ultimate responsibility for Safeguarding within the Church of England. Can she achieve a radical reform of the Church's approach to safeguarding? What might that look like?

My intention here is not to diagnose what is at fault in the Church's systems and practices, as if another review or a bit more tinkering might put things right. Instead, I want to take a step back, think about what abuse is, and what place it has in the life of the Church, as well as thinking carefully about the nature of healing or repair.

Stripping

Abuse happens when a person or organisation uses the power and influence they have to strip away the autonomy of another person. Very often the abuser is trying to make good the deficit they feel within themselves. Any child and any adult is potentially vulnerable to this abuse of power. Harm is done to both the victim and the abuser.

The way that the parable of the Good Samaritan is cast offers an example (Luke 10:25-37). The focus of Jesus' story is *not* on the fact that a man has been beaten-up and stripped by robbers. The violence of the attack is almost glossed over; it is treated as an inevitable fact of life – just the sort of thing that happens on the road from Jerusalem to Jericho. The focus of the story is on the relationships between the wounded victim and the passers-by; representatives of wider society, and especially of the religious community. The pedagogical tremor occurs when we see the inhumanity with which the priest and the Levite treat the victim. Theirs is a one-directional relationship, that takes account only of their own needs. In the first assault, by the thieves, the man is robbed of his property, his clothing, his dignity. Then in the second assault, by the priest and the Levite, he is robbed of his identity, his self-worth and his hope for recovery. This is contrasted with the grace in the relationship between the victim and the Samaritan. The Samaritan is not even described as good. This is simply how two people who meet on the road should treat each other: not with the violence of the robbers, or the superiority of the priest or the disdain of the Levite, but with the mutual grace of the Samaritan and the victim, who give and receive care as equals.

The victim's wounds matter, and they need to be treated. His shame is real, and it needs to be addressed. But Christian theology doesn't suggest that the seriousness of the abuse correlates with its impact, or with the social status of the participants, or with the degree of responsibility of the victim. It's not relevant to ask why the man was walking alone on the road from Jerusalem to Jericho, or whether he was wise to do so. His needs are already complex when he arrives in the story. He is wounded, alone, naked and humiliated. The distinctive aspect of Christian theology is that wounded relationships matter as much if not more than wounded bodies. The priest and the Levite don't just ignore the needs of the victim. The story makes a point of the fact that they see the victim, but make a choice to define themselves against him. They don't even just walk past; they cross the road. In these terms, the priest and the Levite, for all their status and privilege, are the pitiable figures. At least the victim knows his own need. The priest and the Levite never acknowledge their own wounds and their conflicted feelings at seeing a naked, bleeding man. This isn't the Parable of the Good Samaritan; it is the Parable of the Bad Priests.

The nature of abuse is to strip the victim of their personhood. It is a conscious invasion by a person with power, intended to violently challenge and destabilise the physical, sexual, cultural and spiritual identity of someone else. It might involve robbing the victim of their dignity, their reputation, their security or their agency over their own body. It might involve using physical or spiritual force to make them do things they would not choose. In adult victims, it often means making them feel like a child. In children, it often involves taking away the sense of safety or security that allows them to act appropriately for their age. In every case it involves robbing the individual of their legitimate boundaries, so that they feel unwhole. The victim is stripped of his clothes, beaten, and left alone and half-dead.

In abuse, the abuser appropriates a power that does not belong to them, and uses it to say to the victim, '*You are not wholly yourself; you are mine.*' It is a profoundly intimate act; the most fundamental form of identity theft. It is only the stubborn endurance of victims that enables them to survive at all.

What makes abuse in a Christian context particularly grievous is that the identity of every individual is fully realised only in the wounds of Christ. The scandal of Christianity is that the nature of Christ is not power but humility. So for Christians, the wounded victim, not the powerful offender, is the icon of Christ. In the humiliation of abuse, the victim discovers the reality of Christ, and the abuser loses it. It is in the wounds of the victim that the humility of Christ is revealed. A distinctively Christian understanding of abuse needs to take account not only of the distortion of the relationship between two individuals, but also of the relationship between each individual and God. When the victimised individual is forced into a diminished version of their own personhood, the window through which their relationship with God is realised also shrinks. The impact on the abuser is similar. When they take to themselves a status that is greater than that of their victim, their own understanding of God is diminished. The healing of relationships between the abuser, the abused, and God the creator is not only a sacred duty of the Church but a missional task.

Every single human relationship is an encounter between wounded people capable of both good and evil. Abuse occurs whenever a broken person misuses their power to harm another broken person. Repair isn't achieved merely by rebalancing the debts, but by restoring both parties to a relationship of dignity and humility before each other and before God. In my experience many victims of church abuse understand this, and it partly accounts for their enduring longing for the Church to return to a place of humility and justice. Victims own their own brokenness and shame, while the Church and its officers often struggle to do so. The broken victim crying out for justice is a theologian and a prophet whose voice the Church needs to hear. When a wounded victim, robbed of all but the least scrap of their dignity and identity, cries out '*I too am human; and broken as I am, I matter*', she is bringing to the Church a profound lived truth that those who feel the need to project strength desperately need to understand. When the victim stubbornly says to the Church '*You are better than this,*' the Church needs to hear what is being said to it.

Christians ought to understand that the capacity for sin is universal. Abuse is not simply a personality type. It can happen anywhere where human weakness and opportunity coincide. This is why we must pay attention to those aspects of the culture and theology of church life that lend themselves to exploitative relationships.

The uncomfortable truth is that the culture of deference renders the Church institutionally abusive.

The horrific cases of sexual and psychological manipulation that come to public attention are no more than the unacceptable extreme of the continuum of unwarranted privileges embedded in church culture. Mercifully, most clergy and other leaders do not actively abuse the authority they have been given to exploit others. But many do, even in the most subtle ways. 'Power over' rather than 'power with' is baked into the patriarchal ecclesiology of the Church in ways that Christ specifically forbade. Successive generations of Church leaders have refused to recognise this, and consequently failed to engage with the social dynamics of abuse. The reason that abuse has been so persistent in the Church of England is quite simply that the most powerful people in the Church have not been willing to recognise and let go of the trappings of power.

This is what victims mean when they describe the slow, inconsistent and adversarial processes of the Church as re-abusive. The victim on the Jericho Road watches in horror and disbelief as the figures of the priest and the Levite become smaller and smaller in the distance, willing them to turn back and realise their mistake, unable to comprehend that the institution that shaped their personhood no longer chooses to recognise it. She might run after them to reason with them, except that her legs are already broken by the attack. Only when both priest and Levite have finally disappeared over the horizon is the victim confronted with the realisation that they are truly alone.

And then along comes the Samaritan ....

Re-dressing

Bishops and other senior Church leaders find themselves hurrying down the road from Jerusalem to Jericho, under-resourced, with busy agendas to fulfil. As they journey they encounter victims of church abuse, lying naked at the side of the road in obvious distress. The parable could hardly be clearer. Church leaders have a responsibility to stop and attend to victims, even if that creates an inconvenient or embarrassing interruption to their business.

Archbishop Sarah brings relevant experience to this. For five years from 1999 she was Director of Patient Experience for NHS England. One of her concerns in those days was to replace the undignified hospital gowns that were so hated by patients with something that restored self-respect. Now as archbishop, her task is to find ways to re-dress victims of church abuse; to turn them back from patients to persons. Healing the broken is part of our mission as Church. Our job is to reverse the dynamics of the trauma and thus 're-dress' the naked victim – to restore the personhood, dignity and hope they have lost.

We have established that abuse in a church context corrupts the relationship between the victim, the abuser and the institution. That being so, the goal of the Church after abuse has to include the repair of its own relationship with the survivor. The priest and the Levite also need to be re-dressed – not because their robes of office have been stolen from them in the attack, but because by ignoring the victim, they have been stripped of their meaning.

The immediate difficulty here is that the religious leaders haven't arrived on the scene equipped for the situation. They are not experts in helping people to recover from abuse. The priest who meets a victim of abuse might like to see themselves as a bringer of healing, but first they need to recognise that they belong to the same community as the abuser. Any suggestion that the Church can offer the victim a paternal embrace simply reinforces the self-idolatry that enabled the original abuse. That includes patronising assurances that the Church will 'listen to victims' or include 'survivor representatives' in projects – assertions that many victims now find meaningless and patronising. Reconciliation is a gift of God. It can only be received if members and leaders of the Church are able to recognise their own nakedness; to enter into their own wounds, and through them into the pain of the community and of the victim. The task for the Church is not to organise its business so as to seal up or scar over its own wounds, but to sit with them in the presence of Christ until they are transformed by grace. This sitting with the wounds is the first step to repentance, without which no other steps can be made. A Church that cannot bear to look at its own wounds will never be able to offer the restorative grace of God to anyone else. Many well-meaning initiatives in safeguarding polity are flawed because they stem from the same excess of self-importance that leads to abuse in the first place. Any theology of mending must start with God. The wounds of God, voluntarily accepted in Christ, are the only route to healing for the Church.

For years, the Church has balked at this step of dependency. Instead, it has chosen to commit its relationship with victims of abuse to the secular managerialism of safeguarding policies and practices. Well-meaning professionals with barely any concept of the spiritual dimension of church-related abuse, or any overt acknowledgement of the grace of God or the work of prayer, have been charged with organising the Church's offer to victims. For example, most of the Church of England's safeguarding staff are drawn from the police and social services. It is not deemed necessary or desirable that those who minister on the Church's behalf with victims and survivors of abuse should have any personal experience or understanding of Christian faith or spirituality. In many cases they don't even come to the job with an understanding of the mechanics of church life. It is as if the National Health Service had taken people with no experience or understanding of medicine and appointed them as surgeons, issuing scalpels to hospital administrators and prescription pads to personnel managers. This is such a fundamental category error that it almost looks almost like a tactic to avoid bishops having to engaging with the spiritual dimensions of wounding and healing.

It is only out of spiritual brokenness that the Church can begin to meet and embrace the broken victim. Victims of abuse are the premier theologians of a broken Church. They hold up a mirror to the Church saying, *'Look! You too are wounded'*. This is categorically different from other types of injury and healing. The physical injuries of the man attacked on the Jericho Road could be treated so that his physical wounds were healed. If he lost money in the attack, he could be compensated. But the mending of personhood broken by abuse is different. Acts of abuse, once done, cannot be undone. The wounds of abuse cannot be undone by counselling, finance or apologies. An individual whose identity has been radically traumatised by abuse can never be restored to the place they were before the assault. At best they will find a new place of integrity. The aim of healing is not to make amends, but to restore identity and hope for both. A precondition for the Church in enabling healing after abuse is the acknowledgement that it is powerless to achieve it. If the Church allows itself for a moment to imagine that it can undo the damage that has been done, or heal wounded souls, it will immediately fall into the trap of auto-idolatry.

So what is to be done? I'm quite sure that in terms of shame over safeguarding failures, Archbishop Sarah is starting where her predecessor ended. But shame is not enough. It can even be self-indulgent.

The first step in healing the crisis in abuse is for the Church of England to devote very extended time to self-examination and repentance. This is a painful process, but utterly necessary. The secular rush towards 'Lessons Learned' which currently characterises the Church's approach entirely circumvents the most fundamental lesson, which is that the Church is broken beyond its own repair. The most urgent need of the Church in the face of the abuse crisis is not for improved management or training, but for transparency, humility and spiritual leadership that drives it to its knees. Only when the Church enters deeply into its own woundedness will it find Christ waiting there to receive it.

The second step towards mending is for leaders of the Church to draw very close to victims, and devote extended time to listening to them. There is a fragment of a story in Luke's gospel (22:51) that brings me up short every time I read it. It comes in the account of Jesus' arrest in the Garden of Gethsemane. When an armed mob came to arrest Jesus, his disciples grabbed their weapons. Like many of today's Church leaders, they were making a wild effort to regain control of the situation. One of them even struck out with a sword, and lashed out at the mob, cutting off the right ear of the high priest's servant. Jesus spoke sharply to his followers, telling them to put away their weapons. In the midst of the melee, he stopped and touched the ear of the injured servant boy, and healed him.

It's the touching that gets me. You can't heal someone if you are not close enough to touch them. Every time I meet with a person who has been abused in the life of the Church – and I meet them almost every day in the course of my strange vocation – I remember how, in the middle of chaos and threat, Jesus made it his absolute priority to heal the person his disciple had hurt.

One might assume that victims don't want to meet with Church leaders, but the opposite is usually the case. The priest and the Levite will certainly have some explaining to do when they arrive back on the scene. In practice, it is Church leaders who, like the priest and the Levite, seem to find it distasteful to come close to open wounds. The motivation for listening to victims as they show their wounds is not that by doing so, the Church can offer some form of healing. It is the very reverse. The Church needs to attend scrupulously to the wounds of victims for a long time, until it is convinced of its own helplessness.

Many Church leaders fail to understand this role, and act as if, in their dealings with victims, they are being asked vicariously to make good the acts of a previous generation. The contemporary Church and its leaders should take upon themselves the responsibility for the abuse perpetrated by their predecessors, not in order to assuage inherited guilt, nor because they want to save the Church from public disgrace or to reverse its decline, but precisely because Christ is to be discovered in the wounds of the victim. For that reason, the involvement of victims in the process of reconciliation is not a box-ticking exercise but a part of the spiritual journey towards healing for the Church. The wounded victim is the closest neighbour to the wounding Church, and neither can find healing without the other. There is no surer route to the heart of Christ than through the wounds of victims. The first clear sign that restoration is dawning is not the returning health of the victim, but the humility of the Church.

The purpose of redress is to reverse the impact of abuse on the victim. This is what is described in the ordinal as 'the cure of souls'. It can only be achieved by love. Like the oil and wine poured on the victim's wounds, the actions of the attentive Church affirm the worth and identity of the broken victim. The Church needs to be a body that enables survivors to reframe damaged perceptions of themselves.

The Church needs to engage with its victims, not asking how much it needs to do to repay its debts, but with the humility of understanding that it can never do enough.

It will be obvious by now that re-dress cannot be a single event. The damage suffered by a victim might have occurred on a particular day, (though in the vast majority of cases it takes place over an extended period), but the trauma suffered by both victim and abuser is chronic. Re-dress comes only through gentle and consistent attention to the victim. The accounts that I hear from survivors of Church abuse could hardly be more different. One wrote to me recently about their engagement with the Church. 'It feels like I'm approaching an unfeeling, giant monument that I'm legally obligated to engage with. They are a powerful machine; I am a single, broken person. They have the resources and the authority, and I have to perform compliance and gratitude for the crumbs of support, all while knowing they hold the record of how they hurt me. It is a deeply dehumanizing process.'

The Church needs to look for imaginative and bespoke ways of releasing whatever it is that the victim needs to enable them to flourish. That might be information; it might be security in the form of guaranteed housing or sustained income; it might involve public apology or other signs of humility. All of this will be time-consuming and humbling. It will require imagination. It may be costly in ways that insurers cannot comprehend. It will certainly be disturbing for the Church and its leaders.

The crisis of abuse could well be terminal for the

Church of England. Alternatively, Archbishop Sarah could resolve to turn around and lead the Church on the painful journey back up the Jericho Road to meet the victim there, and to begin to re-dress her. If the Church can make that journey, it may begin to rediscover the love of God in brokenness – the brokenness that a victim of abuse shares with every Church leader; the brokenness that the community of the Church embodies and shares with the wider community. And in that discovery, the Church might just find that its own wounds begin to heal, and its own nakedness may be re-dressed.

An earlier version of this chapter was published by the William Temple Foundation in 2022.

PRAYER

God of the wounded and broken,
forgive your Church for the harm we have
 caused to your children.
Strip us of our plans, our privilege and our pride
and direct us back up the road from Jericho
 to Jerusalem
to where we will find you lying wounded at
 the side of the road.
Then give us grace to recognise that we
 are wounded too,
and to share with victims and survivors,
 your precious ones,
the painful journey back towards wholeness.
Amen.

7
Challenge Inequality, Change Practice, Deepen Spirituality

Poverty and the Church of England

Jon Kuhrt

Susie was one of the homeless people you walk past, huddled, sleeping rough in a shop doorway. Growing up in a traveller family where life was tough, she married young to a man who turned out to be violent and abusive. She ran away but got drawn into a chaotic life of drug addiction, criminal behaviour and imprisonment. She said, 'I think the drugs were to block things out ... most of the time I would wish I was dead.'[1]

Tragically, Susie's story is all too familiar. We are living in an era of record homelessness: rough sleeping rose by 20 per cent last year, continuing a post-pandemic trend. Record numbers are homeless and living in temporary accommodation.[2] In London alone, this costs local councils £5.5m every single day.[3] Most shockingly, 1,611 people died homeless in 2024/25.[4]

Thankfully Susie's story did not end this way. Today, she is thriving in supported accommodation run by the Christian homelessness organisation Hope into Action, and is deeply involved in her local community. And the Church of England has been fundamental to her remarkable journey of recovery.

Hope into Action empowers churches to end

homelessness by encouraging people with wealth to invest in houses which we turn into homes. We provide professional Empowerment Workers, and local churches offer friendship and community. Along with foodbanks and debt centres, we are an example of how the church has responded to poverty in new ways over two decades.

After being discharged from prison, Susie was accepted into one of our houses which is linked with Norwich Cathedral, supported by volunteer befrienders Jessica and Nonnie, and Rach, her Empowerment Worker. This support led her to attend regularly her local C of E church, St Catherine's.

As Susie puts it: 'If not for Hope into Action, I wouldn't be alive today. I was giving up on life ... I have a really good life now, all because of my Empowerment Worker and my church community.'

Susie is not just a recipient of the help of others, she is a *contributor* to the life of the local church community and has been able to help support other families affected by addictions. Earlier this year, she even ran a 5k race to raise funds for Hope into Action, which led her to quit smoking, having been a smoker for 54 years.

Most significantly, she chose to be baptised: 'The day of my baptism was really cold, but as soon as I got out of the water, I felt a warm feeling come over me. I'm glad I made the commitment.'

Understanding poverty

Stories like Susie's illustrate both the current nature of UK poverty *and* the unique role the Church of England can play in helping people. In this chapter I would like to outline three fundamental underlying causes of poverty, and to recommend three principal directions for the Church of England under Archbishop Sarah's leadership in the years ahead.

The Church needs a holistic understanding of poverty because accurate diagnosis informs effective action. Just as homelessness is more than lack of accommodation, poverty is more than lack of material assets.

For over 20 years I have used this three-way analysis as I reflect on poverty I have witnessed and worked to address. Whilst these three factors are seen *in extremis* within homelessness, they are evident in all deprived communities across the UK.

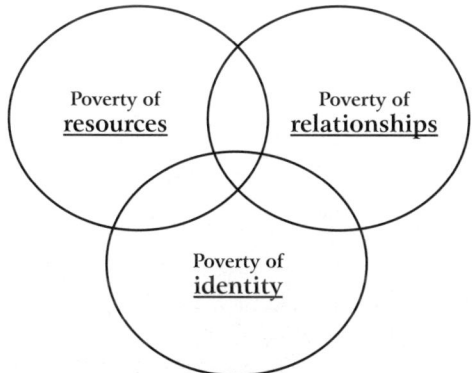

Firstly, the **poverty of resources**. Susie came from a materially poor community, and the most obvious factor in contemporary poverty is material deprivation driven by the increasing cost of living, rising debt, unemployment, under-employment, and insecure zero-hours work.

In 2025, the Joseph Rowntree Foundation reports that over 21 per cent of the UK population are living in poverty: 8.1 million working-age adults, 4.3 million children, and 1.9 million pensioners.[5] Over 25 years the number in very deep poverty has grown by around two-thirds.[6] In-work poverty has increased: in 2022/23, 63 per cent of children and working-age adults in poverty lived in families where at least one adult was working part-time or more, up from 56 per cent in 2012/13 and 44 per cent in 1996/97.[7]

Organisations like Trussell with its network of foodbanks (77 per cent church-based) and Christians Against Poverty's Debt Centres have grown rapidly in response to this rise in poverty.

But whilst material poverty is most obvious, the problem runs deeper.

Secondly, the **poverty of relationships**. All stories of homelessness involve broken relationships: often people have *nowhere* to go because they have *no one* to go to.

In Susie's story, domestic violence triggered her homelessness. Such abuse traumatises people in far-reaching, destructive ways.

This is why family fragility is so relevant to poverty: when the safety net provided by a loving family frays, more people fall through it. The Centre for Social Justice's research shows that among 5-10-year-olds, 6 per cent of children with married parents experienced diagnosable mental health issues compared to 12 per cent with cohabiting parents, and 18 per cent with a lone parent.[8]

Thirdly and most deeply, the **poverty of identity**. It is not just relationships with *others* but with *themselves* which is often fragile. We are living in a time of epidemic low self-esteem, anxiety and mental health problems which affect people's ability to work and make ends meet.

For Susie and countless others, addictions are driven by the need for distraction, a form of self-medication to deal with emotional pain and trauma. This poverty of identity undermines someone's very sense of self: an *inner* poverty far harder to change than external needs.

This three-way model shows why homelessness

is much more than houselessness: houses are vital *resources* but homes are places of *relationship* and *identity*.

Dynamically interconnected

Homelessness is the end result of these different aspects of poverty dynamically interconnecting: the poverty of resources puts pressure on relationships. Relationship breakdown affects the resources you can access. And relational poverty damages your sense of identity.

Susie's story illustrates this. Addictions rob people of resources, destroy relationships and scar identity. And her transformation addressed each form of poverty: the *resource* of accommodation and *relationships* through church friendship have enabled her to transform her *identity*.

Poverty *is* driven chiefly by economic inequality and unjust allocation of resources. Housing is the starkest example of social injustice: both state and market have comprehensively failed to deliver the affordable, fair housing our country needs.

But poverty is not *limited* to material factors. Addressing it involves more than allocating resources. This is why meaningful employment is so central to fighting poverty. Fair pay is critical, but a good job does more than provide the resource of a wage. It provides relational links to colleagues and teammates in collective endeavour and builds an individual's positive identity through giving meaning and purpose.

Humans are created for meaningful work and we have needs that cannot be met by material resources: we do not live by bread alone. The Church has a vital role in helping address all three aspects of poverty.

The Church of England and poverty

All discussions of poverty are inevitably political. This model I have outlined brings together contrasting political emphases: the left tends to ascribe poverty to structural causes and resource distribution; the right focuses more on relationships, families and individuals.

Forty years ago, this tension was front-page news when the Church of England published the *Faith in the City* report on urban poverty. The report angered the ruling Conservative government and sparked a national debate. Within the Church, John Root offered thoughtful critique:

'There is no greater enemy of wholesome moral debate than polarisation into strongly personal, socially conservative responses; and impersonal, strongly political ones. By contrast scripture constantly interweaves personal holiness and political responsibility ... the Church of England must learn to unite the voices of collective responsibility and personal transformation.'[9]

This polarisation remains a key challenge today. But Christian faith calls us to speak and act against *both* the sin besieging individual lives and the structures blighting whole communities.

The opportunity for the Church is to challenge this polarisation by being faithful to scripture by 'interweaving personal holiness and political responsibility'. To speak prophetically, Christian witness must challenge the echo chambers of left and right.

This requires bravery and risk taking. It may mean losing friends and causing offence, as Jesus warned (Luke 21:12-19). But here, in this tension and synthesis, the Christian gospel's social impact comes alive.

Three directions for Archbishop Sarah

Rising from registered nurse to Chief Nursing Officer for England, Archbishop Sarah brings a unique perspective to addressing poverty through decades of nursing and public health service. Just spend time in any Accident and Emergency waiting room and you will see evidence of what she will know well: that poverty manifests not just in empty pockets but in damaged bodies, traumatised minds, and broken relationships. She has seen first-hand in hospital wards and clinics what I have described here: that poverty is the complex interplay of material deprivation, relational breakdown and personal trauma.

In addition, Archbishop Sarah's experience is in sharp contrast to other senior clerics who only have academic or ecclesiastical experience. Rather than merely diagnosing problems theoretically, she has spent her career implementing practical solutions within complex systems.

This background equips her particularly well for the three directions I outline below. Her experience of leadership in the NHS demonstrates she understands how to engage powerful institutions whilst remaining credible and constructive – vital for speaking prophetically about economic justice. Furthermore, she understands the importance of empowerment, dignity and the dangers of dependency - and knows instinctively why the 'contributory principle' matters. And her willingness to integrate her Christian faith openly within public service equips her to resist the secular trajectory of the Church's social witness or its reduction to mere service delivery.

My hope for Archbishop Sarah is her leadership will refuse to accept the false polarisations between the personal and political, between compassion and justice and between practical action and prophetic witness.

I will set out three directions where I hope Archbishop Sarah will lead a more radical social witness against poverty. Each relates to the three poverty types and connects to Micah's injunction to God's people.

'What does the LORD require? To act justly, love mercy and walk humbly with your God' (Micah 6:8):

1. *Act justly*: **challenging inequality and economic power**
   The growth of Christian social action should provoke questions about social injustice and the economic power which *underlies* such inequality. The gap between rich and poor continues to grow, with the top fifth owning two-thirds of the wealth, and the bottom fifth only 0.5 per cent.[10]

   The housing crisis and unaffordability of decent accommodation highlights the fundamental structural injustice of UK housing. These are not problems which can be solved by voluntary action alone.

   The Church should never accept being the 'handmaid' of the state, filling gaps caused by government neglect and market failure. We must not be seduced by the lure of feeling useful or the superiority that can come from being benefactors to the poor. These tendencies exacerbate class division.

   Rather the Church should stand in solidarity with those trapped in poverty and together demand an economy generating decent, dignified employment. People should not be reduced to mere 'units of labour', manipulated for profit. Our country needs affordable accommodation and work that pays and gives dignity.

2. *Love mercy:* **changing the Church's social action practice**
   The hard reality is that not all responses to poverty are helpful or effective. US Christian activist Robert Lupton argues that too often social action

creates dependency: 'When we do for those in need what they have the capacity to do for themselves, we disempower them.' He distinguishes between *crisis* situations and *chronic* problems: 'An emergency response to chronic need is at best counterproductive and, over time, actually harmful.'[11]

This is a problem in UK Christian responses to poverty. I have visited too many centres where well-meaning middle-class people are running around serving those who are turned into passive recipients.

Too much social action, sometimes called 'mercy ministries', has focused on giving out resources rather than building mutuality. We need models with empowerment and reciprocity at their heart, enabling people trapped in poverty to have agency. A relational rather than transactional approach is fundamental: people need environments where their *contribution* is vital to the change happening.

In food poverty initiatives, beneficiaries should contribute *something* towards provision and have the opportunity to serve others. In homelessness services, this means empowering people to pay rent and playing the lead role in their own recovery.

Christian social action should welcome people into participating in community rather than keeping them in receiving mode. People are transformed through what they participate in and contribute to, not primarily through what they receive free. As well the *grace* of kindness and generosity, we also need to embody the *truth* of challenge and empowerment.

This is *the contributory principle*: all social action should empower beneficiaries to contribute to their own welfare and the well-being of others.

3. ***Walk humbly with God:* deepen the commitment to Christian distinctiveness**

   One of the constant issues I have witnessed in my engagement in social action over the last 30 years is how so many Christian organisations and church-based projects. slide into secularism.

   Sometimes faith *fades* due to a lack of passion or confidence. Sometimes it is due to *fear* about what funders think. Sometimes it becomes *fossilised* when the founding inspiration is neglected.

   It means that rather than something dynamic and creative, faith often becomes just a slightly embarrassing footnote in the history of an organisation. To use Paul Bickley's milk metaphor in *The Problem of Proselytism*,[12] too often faith is 'skimmed out' of social action and it becomes disconnected from the motivations which started it.

   I have spent most of my working life at the skimmed and semi-skimmed end of social action, but I felt called and excited to work for Hope into Action *because* of their full-fat approach. We make no secret of our enthusiasm for integrating passionate faith within a professional working practice.

   Faith in Christ is our *engine:* it's what motivates our investors, donors and staff and what motivates churches to offer friendship and community to our tenants. And as we have seen with Susie's story, faith is so relevant to the recovery journey that so many of our tenants are on. In 2024/25, 60 per cent of our tenants wanted to be prayed for and 14 were baptised or made a formal commitment to Christ.

   Christian social action must maintain its distinctive character because these are built on foundational beliefs about what it means to be human. We are relational beings made in the image of the Almighty God. Relationships are at the heart of what it means to be human because relationships are at the core of a Trinitarian God of Father, Son and Holy Spirit. Our work should *reflect* divine grace and truth and not *reject* it.

The challenging times call for bold witness – not for shy Christianity.

Hope for the future

The depth and challenge of UK poverty and inequality is sobering and the challenges facing Archbishop Sarah are formidable. She will be leading the established Church through a complex situation where there will be continual tensions with the political establishment. We may not have cause for optimism – but we must be people of hope.

And there are reasons for hope. The Church has shown remarkable creativity and responsiveness over the past two decades. Organisations like Christians Against Poverty and Hope into Action demonstrate what can happen when passionate faith meets practical action. Thousands of churches across the country are making a tangible difference in their communities. Stories like Susie's show that transformation is possible when all three dimensions of poverty are addressed together.

Christian efforts to reduce poverty should resist being co-opted into the state-funded 'third sector' and losing our authentic Christian character. We should aim for a more radical witness: to shake the status quo through a bold political voice, rooted in practical action and prayerful discipleship.

Being prophetic involves holding together and integrating that which the world cannot: justice, mercy and walking humbly with God. We need to be willing to challenge across the accepted boundaries of theological echo chambers and political tribalism.

We should not settle for sticking-plaster solutions. We need a holistic understanding of the poverty that plagues our nation – one that calls for both structural change and personal responsibility, that addresses both the political economy and family life, that is both prophetic and practical, and that speaks of both justice and Jesus.

For the gospel must transform individuals if it is to transform society. The Church's social and political impact is derivative because it ultimately relies on people's encounter with the risen Lord Jesus and being willing to participate in communities that express this belief. Authentic faith is always personal, but never private.

In Archbishop Sarah, the Church of England has a leader with a unique background. Let's hope and pray that her combination of professional experience, practical compassion and robust faith offers a model for the kind of integrated Christian witness our country desperately needs.

[1] Susie Mayhew Restore Hope this Easter, Hope into Action video 2025, www.hopeintoaction.org.uk
[2] 20% rise in annual snapshot count of people sleeping rough, Ministry of Housing, Communities and Local Government (MHCLG)
[3] London Councils, 2025
[4] Museum of Homelessness, October 2025
[5] Joseph Rowntree Foundation, *UK Poverty 2025: The essential guide to understanding poverty in the UK*
[6] JRF, *UK Poverty 2025*
[7] The Health Foundation, In-work poverty trends, 2024
[8] The Centre for Social Justice
[9] *Taking on Faith in the City* (Grove Books,1986)
[10] The Equality Trust, *The Scale of Economic Inequality in the UK*, 2025
[11] Robert D. Lupton, *Toxic Charity: How Churches and Charities Hurt Those They Help*
[12] *The Problem of Proselytism* by Paul Bickley, Theos, 2015

PRAYER

Lord God,
Remind your Church of what is *truly* good.
 Convict us of what you require.
We pray for all those whose lives are blighted
 by poverty in our country and our local
 communities.
Give your Church holy anger to seek **justice**,
 loving hearts to be **merciful**, and the
 humility to walk with you in all we do.
We pray for Archbishop Sarah as she leads the
 Church of England. Grant her wisdom,
 courage and grace for the challenges ahead.
Help your Church bring wholeness in place of
 want, hope instead of despair and to do
 this all in the transforming name of Jesus.
Amen.

8
Hopes and Opportunities for the World

Climate Care and the Church of England

Ruth Valerio

'What was the place like where you grew up?', I ask the group of people in front of me. 'And what is different about it now?'

I am standing in front of a group of folks, seated around tables, in an upstairs room. If I turn round and look out of the window behind me, I can see Canterbury Cathedral, standing in all its vast magnificence, its pale golden walls gleaming in the sunlight.

I am here meeting with new bishops from across the Anglican Communion. Every year, Canterbury Cathedral brings together those who have recently become bishops for a week of reflection, teaching and learning from each other, and meeting with the Archbishop. For a few years I have been part of the programme and have done sessions with them looking at the climate and environmental crises.

I watch them as they chat around their tables on the question of what changes they have seen to the place where they grew up. The conversations get animated. I see some people take out their phones and show pictures to the others. Everyone is listening intently to whoever is speaking; nodding in agreement, frowning in sympathy, trying not to interrupt when they have things they want to say too.

After a while I call them back together and we hear some of the things people have been sharing. A bishop from an African country tells us about the village he comes from. He has happy memories of playing in the river with his friends and siblings when he was a boy, catching fish. Now the river has totally gone. The lack of rain has dried it up and killed the fish. Another bishop from the Pacific Islands speaks about the beautiful beaches he loved when he was a child. They are part of his culture and the communal sense of identity. Now when he goes to the beaches he sees plastic everywhere, piling up along the shoreline and floating on the surface of the once pristine waters. A bishop from the United States talks about the woodland that she and her friends used to play in on the edge of her town, with its huge trees and the beautiful colours of the leaves in the autumn. But that wood is now gone too, cut down for a new shopping mall. A bishop from a South East Asian country talks about how many more typhoons there are from when he was a boy and the impact that is having on his home region, and another from a South American country tells us about the beautiful land he comes from and the rich biodiversity he enjoyed when he was a boy. The land has now all been cleared for grazing cattle and the abundance of animals and birds he used to love has gone.

I wonder what has changed for you too if you think about where you grew up? My parents lived in the same house about twenty miles north of London for fifty-four years and they talk about clouds of butterflies in the garden and nearby fields. When I was a child I used to love walking through those fields and to the farm which had pigs and cows as well as arable farming. I would take a book and some sandwiches, sit in the big barn on the bales of hay and talk to the cows and their wide-eyed calves. Over the years some of the fields were built on for a housing development and the farm got rid of its pigs and cows to focus on intensively farming cereal crops. All the butterflies have disappeared and, whilst now a stunning bright yellow with oil seed rape flowers, the land is almost devoid of wildlife.

As the bishops talk, I then ask them to share how environmental crises are impacting their churches and church members. I expect just two or three folks to say something and then I am planning on moving into my main session, but to my surprise there is lots they want to say! People in many of their churches are facing serious challenges as the changing weather patterns are pushing them deeper into poverty. The bishops talk about the huge problem of plastic which is accumulating in the streets and on fields, blocking rivers, causing flooding and increased disease. A bishop from Canada talks about an unprecedented flood that hit her town and destroyed the church, carrying away the bishop's chair. People talk about food deserts, about rising levels of obesity impacting their congregations' health, whilst others talk about failing crops and the ever-present fear of hunger which keeps people away from church meetings. The bishop from the Pacific Islands speaks movingly about the impact on his congregation of the rising seas and salination of crop lands: people are scared, the coral reefs that protect the fish they depend on for food are dying, his church members worry about the future and are leaving the islands. Another bishop talks frustratingly about the political context they are in and how divided her congregation is about whether climate change is even a problem or not.

I have only intended these questions to be an introduction to get the bishops thinking. My time is tight and I need to get on with the teaching I've prepared, but it is clear I have touched a nerve and the things that people are sharing are heartbreaking to listen to. Every region of the world is represented in this room – including Europe and the UK – and every person has something to say about how their churches and congregations are being impacted, whether they come from an economically poorer or wealthier nation. The atmosphere in the room is one of deep listening, of empathy and grieving for what we are hearing and I know I cannot go baldly into my next session. So we pause and take time to acknowledge what we have been hearing, to lament together and pray for our different situations.

※

I am delighted to have been asked to contribute a chapter to this book on Archbishop Sarah Mullally and the ten key challenges that face the Church of England. For some thirty years now I have been writing and speaking on issues of environmental care and social justice: helping churches see how these areas are fundamental aspects of our Christian faith, not optional extras, and trying to give the Church practical resources to live this out, as well as trying to live it out in my own life as best I can (imperfectly). I have done this very much standing on the shoulders of giants: Christian leaders who have been pioneers scientifically and theologically.

For many years I have carried a vision to see the Church change so that it becomes as commonplace for a church to be actively caring for the natural world and its inhabitants – locally and globally – as it is for a church to be involved with running food banks or toddler groups, Bible studies, prayer meetings or evangelistic courses. Over the years I have seen this vision slowly beginning to become reality. It has been exciting seeing the growth of A Rocha UK's Eco Church with around 9,000 registered churches at the time of writing, over 4,500 of whom have a bronze or silver award and over 100 of whom are now gold award holders. Every Church of England and Church in Wales cathedral, bar seven, is registered with Eco Church and forty-three have gained an award.

I remember launching the accompanying Eco Diocese scheme at a Bishops' Breakfast in Oxford and persuading a couple of brave bishops to sign up their diocese then as part of the publicity, in the nervous hope of encouraging others to do the same. Now, thirty-four dioceses have a bronze award and one has silver. Every diocese has a net zero officer, providing support and encouragement to churches and diocesan institutions as they work to transition away from fossil fuels and reduce their emissions.

The Church of England has made really good progress, and other parts of the Anglican Communion are ahead of us, so be encouraged every one of you reading this who has played a part in that. But there is so much more to do and we must not lose our focus or give up.

The stark reality is that, environmentally, things are getting worse. The scientific consensus is that we are heading for a 2.6 degree warmer world, which is catastrophic. Jamaica has been hit by its worst storm ever and the Philippines had to evacuate nearly 1.5 million people when it faced a super typhoon. Iran faces an unprecedented drought with its President saying the capital city Tehran may need to be evacuated. In countries across the world, people are being pushed further into poverty because of the changing climate which has knock-on sociological impacts on areas such as education, child marriage and domestic violence. We are not immune in the UK either: three of the five worst harvests on record in England have occurred this decade following periods of extreme weather. In this period we have had both the wettest spring and the driest spring on record - both manifestations of climate change Our cost-of-living crisis is in large part due to rising global food prices because of climate change, and rising fossil fuel prices after Russia's invasion of Ukraine. It is our reliance on fossil fuels rather than net zero actions that is causing us problems.

This is not just an emergency we have to get through: this is an existential threat that will eventually engulf us all. It is wider than climate change too, though of course everything is interlinked. It is not an overstatement to say we are destroying our planet and many of the beautiful creatures that share it with us. There is now no part of our world that does not bear the imprints of our lack of care in some way, whether through the changing climate or plastic waste, overfishing, pollution, habitat loss, biodiversity decline and more besides.

So why should this matter to Archbishop Sarah, the Church of England and indeed the wider Anglican Communion? Because, alongside this being possibly the biggest challenge we face as a species, it is also a huge opportunity. As Sarah steps into her new role, she has a wonderful opportunity to lead prophetically and powerfully in this area; to present a fresh vision and even a fresh spirituality, and to mobilise the worldwide Anglican community to deeper action and thereby to deeper engagement in living out the good news – the Gospel – of Jesus Christ.

Specifically, I want to offer three reasons why this area is so vital for her and us to engage with.

First, because it goes right to the heart of our Christian faith

Caring for the wider natural world – including but not limited to taking action on climate – is not an optional extra but a fundamental part of what the good news of Jesus Christ is about. As the first line of our Bibles and the first line of our creed states, we believe in a God who has created the heavens and the earth: i.e. everything ('the heavens and the earth' being a kind of catch-all phrase). This world comes from the very breath – the *ruach* – of God, and all creatures have God's breath in them. This world is not something rubbish to be destroyed: it is infused with the very presence of God. And God cares deeply about all aspects of God's creation, not only the human part. Job 39 and several psalms speak of God's loving care. If the God we worship loves this world so much, do we not also want to love and treat it well as part of our worship and discipleship?

Our faith is rooted in Jesus. In his incarnation, life, crucifixion and resurrection we see a strong affirmation of the created order. In the incarnation, Jesus not only became a human being, he became flesh – *sarx* – entering into the whole created order. In his life we see someone who is grounded in the natural world – just take a moment to think about all the plants, soils, animals, birds that feature in his teaching. The apostle Paul tells us clearly that Jesus' blood shed on the cross was for *all things on earth and in heaven*, not only for people (Colossians 1:20, and see 2 Corinthians 5:19). And in the resurrection we see an affirmation of the bodily, physical realm and a prefiguration of the future transformed heavens and earth which, like Jesus' body, will carry both continuity and discontinuity.[1]

The God of the Trinity is intricately involved with and loves the creation and provides a pattern for us to follow.[2] We are made in God's image and are called to represent God to the wider creation; we are created to be the species that takes care of the rest of what God has made. Our Scriptures show us that this earth – blue and green – is not just an object for exploration and use, but is intrinsically very good, worthy of being saved, and thus to be respected and shared for the common good.

The second reason why climate action and environmental care matters is because they intersect with many other issues, including some of the other chapters in this book

In the Anglican Communion's Five Marks of Mission, the fifth is, 'To strive to safeguard the integrity of creation, and sustain and renew the life of the earth', with the others being:

1. To proclaim the Good News of the Kingdom
2. To teach, baptise and nurture new believers
3. To respond to human need by loving service
4. To transform unjust structures of society, to challenge violence of every kind and pursue peace and reconciliation.

I would contend that whole creation care is integral to all the marks of mission and cannot be restricted only to a final point at the end. The good news of the Kingdom is an emaciated gospel and does not represent the fullness of the biblical vision of the Kingdom if it does not include the whole created order.[3] Similarly, we must ensure that our discipleship of new believers is holistic and includes the call to care for God's world, and we need to equip believers to deal with the world they live in, giving them much-needed faith tools to navigate a world facing an existential threat.

We cannot respond to human need without seeing the wider environmental context within which that need occurs and without recognising how poverty and ecological breakdown are so inextricably linked, here in the UK too, not only in other countries. And our work against systemic injustice and violence likewise must hold together the human and the ecological. Genocide and ecocide go terrifyingly hand-in-hand, as I witness awfully through my work with Embrace the Middle East.[4]

Issues of climate and ecological breakdown do not stand separately to other issues. The intersectionalities are vast and, once you gain some level of ecological literacy, you see the interweaving right across societal structures. We cannot care about people and poverty without caring about the land people live on, the seas they fish in, the air they breathe, the food they eat … and vice versa. We cannot care about issues of gender and race and not care about the climate crisis which impacts indigenous women, black women and women of colour more than any other person. We cannot care about health and wellbeing without seeing the huge role played by environmental factors, both positively and negatively. We cannot care about the rise of the far right and Christian Nationalism without being prepared to tackle their negative narratives around 'net zero' and without recognising that the ecological crisis (as a factor in itself and as a contributor to conflict) is one of the main reasons why people are forced to leave their homes and seek asylum elsewhere.

The third reason why these issues matter is because they are an integral part of our mission

I want to state absolutely clearly that – even whilst recognising that resources are tight and have to be managed carefully – caring for the natural world, going for an Eco Church award and working for net zero ambitions are not in competition with the mission of the Church, but are part of a wider whole. Indeed one of the wonderful things I have observed over the years is that churches that engage more in ecological issues often attract more people from their local community and see people coming to faith.

Despite what the mainstream media might want us to think, the vast majority of people care deeply about what is happening to the climate and nature. Research shows that 89 per cent of the world's people want stronger action to fight the climate crisis but feel they are trapped in a self-fulfilling 'spiral of silence' because they mistakenly believe they are in a minority.[5] That depth of care means many people are also very worried about the state of the ecological world and want to see action being taken. Ecological grief and anxiety are now well recognised psychological states that many of us carry, though I suspect most of us keep those feelings tucked away, sometimes because of that 'spiral of silence' and often because the pain is simply too much to acknowledge too often. Climate or ecological anxiety are impacting young people in particular as they face an uncertain future and a world that will look very different to the world of their grandparents. A global study found that 45 per cent of young people globally feel climate anxiety negatively impacts their lives and almost two-thirds (64 per cent) believe governments are not doing enough to protect them from the impacts of the climate crisis.[6]

A Church that is silent and actionless on these issues is irrelevant to many it is trying to reach, and, if the Church wants to grow younger, then it needs to take seriously the things that young people care about – which include environmental issues and climate change.[7]

Engaging in environmental action is also a wonderful way to build common ground with others. Speaking into the chapter on global Anglican unity, as we saw with our bishops earlier, the impact of the climate crisis and the need for action is one thing we can all stand together on and that can draw us together rather than tear us apart. It takes us across the ecumenical divides as well and is a great way to work with other faiths. One of the pleasures for me in developing and leading Eco Church was then working with Rabbi Jonathan Wittenberg to launch Eco Synagogue. In addition, many Anglicans and other Christians reach deeply into secular activist, business and political groups and this gives us opportunities to build constructive relationships which can prove beneficial for addressing other issues too. We all share one common home and we need to look after it together.

So, five hopes that I have for Archbishop Sarah and for all of us:

First, build a positive, hopeful vision of the future

I want to see Sarah leading a conversation and speaking out on what kind of society we want to live in. What kind of people do we want to be? What are the values we want to be known by: as Anglicans, as Christians in general and for all of us, whatever faith we do or do not hold? Personally, I want to live in a place where car pollution does not exacerbate my asthma. I want the air to be clear and the waterways clean so I and my children can swim in them without fear of getting ill. I want my city to be full of green: flowers and wild verges for beauty and insects; plants for foraging and health; trees to provide shade, shelter for others and to bring the temperature down during heatwaves. I want nature and her wild creatures to be flourishing around me. I want our food to come from systems that help people and planet to be healthy. Who would not want all those things?! I want us to live by values of love, compassion, peace, welcome, hope. I want us to stand against the loud voices of consumerism and to be content with what we have; to know that true wealth and happiness does not come from having more things or flying to more exotic places.[8]

The good news is that there *is* a lot of good news! Whilst not diminishing the realities of the challenges we face, I am constantly humbled and inspired by how many brilliant people there are in the UK and all around the world, who are doing amazing things to care for this fragile but beautiful world in more ways than we can possibly imagine. And we are making progress. China looks set to hit its target of peak CO_2 emissions well ahead of schedule. Green energy now provides more electricity than coal in Australia and the UK is a world leader in off-shore wind energy. There are also countless numbers of Christians and churches – including Anglican churches – in every region of the world, taking action and showing how to integrate whole creation care into their church lives. [9] Perhaps our biggest challenge is holding despair and hope together at the same time.

Secondly, make the most of the great resources that are out there

If we care about these issues and our responsibility towards our neighbour and the earth, then we will want to take action and that means taking responsibility for our emissions; investing in our buildings to make them fit for our future; speaking out prophetically to governments and businesses; addressing the underlying spiritual causes of the problems in terms of selfishness, greed and over-consumption.

A Rocha UK, Christian Aid, Christian Climate

Action, diocesan environmental officers, Green Christian, Operation Noah, Tearfund [rv5] all have brilliant resources to help with these things and more, with Eco Church being the obvious place to start. Your net zero diocesan officer will be able to give you excellent advice on your church and keep an eye on the Church of England website for a very good resource that is being worked on at the time of writing this chapter, coming from the Faith and Order Commission.

Anglican churches are, by dint of the parish system, at the heart of communities and ideally placed to be a force for good and to bring hope locally, so make the most of the excellent resources that can help you do that.

Thirdly, for Archbishop Sarah specifically: please do something proactive as you come into role that makes it clear you believe climate action and whole creation care are part of the DNA of the Church

More creative people than me will have better ideas (feel free dear readers to bombard Lambeth Palace with suggestions!), but a basic would be to do a carbon, meat or plastic fast for Lent. I would encourage then doing a more positive eco-feast during the Season of Creation (running from 1 September, the World Day of Prayer for Creation, to the Feast of St Francis of Assisi on 4 October), during which Sarah does something positive for nature every day or every Sunday.

Fourthly, encourage a fresh Christian nature spirituality

We are part of a world that sings God's praises; a world that is alive with God's presence, 'charged with the grandeur of God', that will flame out, 'like shining from shook foil'.[i] The world is not something God made from a distance, like waving a magic wand or carving up the body of a defeated goddess, as the Babylonian creation narrative would have it. No, the world comes from inside of God's own self, so to speak, and thus she is suffused with God's presence. That does *not* mean that the creation *is* God, but it does strongly indicate a much greater closeness between God and God's creation than our Christian theology has often allowed.[ii]

This has been recognised in Christian theology through the ages, but we have become afraid of that way of thinking due to a right desire to avoid 'New Age' influences. However we have taken that too far and separated humanity from the wider creation in ways that are unhelpful to us environmentally and spiritually. I was struck by a church leader saying to me, embarrassed, 'I confess I find God more in nature than in my church'. I thought, 'Why is finding God in nature something to be confessed? Of course you do – this is God's creation!' So there is a Christian creational spirituality we need to discover that recovers the closeness and connectedness between God and God's creation and our place within that, and that brings this ecological conversion into our theological and liturgical life.[10]

Finally, fifthly, do not be afraid to speak out politically

It is essential that we are acting to reduce our emissions and take care of the natural world in our churches and our individual lives, but, we also need to call governments and businesses to take action on a larger, systemic scale. We can all be doing this – joining with the organisations mentioned above in the campaigns they run – and Archbishop Sarah will have a particular role in standing against the current political trend towards far-right post-truth climate denialism and building confidence that working towards net zero is the right and best way to go, for everyone and everything.

She will receive criticism, of course, and will be told to stay in the box of personalised religion. But the Church of England, with Sarah at its head, needs to be forthright and unequivocal in stating that working for a stable climate & the care of God's wonderful creation is integral to leadership for the global common good, and unafraid to confront leaders who abuse power and public trust through irresponsible and reckless climate governance.

Three reasons why climate and environment should matter to Archbishop Sarah and the Anglican Church. Five hopes I have as she steps into role. Let's put those hopes into action!

1. I have packed a vast amount of biblical theology into two paragraphs here! To unpack it, please read R. Valerio, *Saying Yes to Life* (SPCK: 2019). You will also find helpful, D. Bookless, *Planetwise: Dare to care for God's world* (IVP: 2008) and R. Parry, *Christian Eco-Spirituality: An Outline* (Cascade Books: 2025)
2. I am aware I have not touched on the role of the Spirit here. For a short introduction, see: https://ruthvalerio.net/bibletheology/a-trinitarian-approach-to-the-climate-crisis-part-3-the-perfecting-holy-spirit/
3. See, https://ruthvalerio.net/bibletheology/gospel-whole-gospel-nothing-gospel/.
4. See www.embraceme.org .
5. https://www.theguardian.com/environment/2025/apr/22/activate-climate-silent-majority-support-supercharge-action
6. Climate anxiety in children and young people and their beliefs about government responses to climate change: a global survey Hickman, Caroline et al. The Lancet Planetary Health, Volume 5, Issue 12, e863 - e873.
7. See this report from Tearfund and Youthscape: https://

8. www.tearfund.org/-/media/tearfund/files/tearfund-speakers/ys_tf_bdth_report_full5.pdf
9. To explore how we live well as followers of Jesus in our consumer culture, see, R. Valerio, *Just Living: Faith and community in an age of consumerism* (Hodder Faith: 2018).
9. For lots of inspiring examples, see, *Saying Yes to Life*.
10. For more on this see chapter six of, R. Valerio, *How to Survive a World in Crisis (And not give up doing good)* (SPCK:2026), and R. Parry, *Christian Eco-Spirituality: An Outline*. And see also the outdoor worship materials from Engage Worship and the examples of the Hazelnut Community network, Magdalene Community Church in the NE of England, Forest Church, and a network of churches involved in outdoor worship (https://www.facebook.com/profile.php?id=61550013325543).
i See Gerard Manley Hopkins, 'God's Grandeur'.
ii R. Valerio, *Saying Yes to Life*, 35.

PRAYER
Contributed by Revd Jon Swales

Father of Creation,
whose breath moves through river and reef,
soil and skin,
we lift before you Sarah Mullally,
your servant,
who holds the key of high office,
yet remains frail flesh in a complex world,
called to lead your Church
in the age of great unravelling.

You have placed her in a world
that groans beneath the weight
of our excess.
We come alongside her
with what we've broken,
what we've burned,
what we still long to love.

Temperatures rise.
Emissions still climb.
The seas swell.
Storms strike harder.
Crops wither.
The balance shifts.
And creation cries out.

This crisis falls heaviest
on the poor,
the uprooted,
those already pushed to the edge.

Give Sarah prophetic courage
to speak when silence is rewarded,
to resist denial and delay,

to reject every gospel
that forgets the earth
or severs justice from praise.

Root her hope in the Crucified and Risen One:
a hope wide enough for lament,
stubborn enough to endure,
bold enough to be enacted.
Teach her to listen
across borders and cultures,
to stories held in scar tissue,
to silence heavy with fear,
to futures already trembling.

We pray that Sarah would lead
with ears tuned to sorrow,
a heart open to wonder,
and hands ready for costly love.

Lead her and lead us
into deeper repentance,
towards a faith that tends the land,
a mission that mends injustice,
a Church brave enough to bless
all of creation.

By your Spirit,
lead Sarah in fierce hope.
By your Spirit,
lead us in holy defiance.

Through Sarah's faithful witness
and through ours,
may your Church become
a sign of costly compassion
for the displaced,
the forgotten,

and the more-than-human world,
until justice rolls
in the reconciliation of all things.

Amen.

9
The Thread that Binds Us
The Challenge of Global Anglican Unity
Amatu Christian-Iwuagwu

Introduction: A Communion at a Crossroads

The Anglican Communion stands at a defining moment in its long and remarkable story. Spread across more than 165 countries, encompassing more than 85 million believers, we are a global fellowship united not by legal compulsion but by a shared inheritance of worship, mission, and relationship. Ours is a communion bound together – sometimes loosely, sometimes painfully – by what the Lambeth Conference has described as 'the bonds of affection'. These bonds have been stretched by cultural change, theological disagreement, and political complexity. Yet they remain intact, a testament to the Spirit's persistent work among us.

The approaching installation of Archbishop Sarah, the first woman to hold the office of Archbishop of Canterbury, adds historic significance to this moment. Her leadership arrives not simply as a change of personnel but as an invitation to re-imagine the Anglican family, to rediscover the heart of communion, and to walk together with renewed hope.

My own journey – from being born into the chaos of the Nigerian Civil War, to ministry in diverse English parishes, to leadership within the Church of England, General Synod, and the Church Commissioners – has taught me that unity is rarely easy. It is a spiritual struggle, a discipline of the heart, and a work of God. My Igbo name, *Iheanyichukwu* – 'nothing is impossible with God' – is not a romantic motto but a theological conviction forged in survival, calling, and mission.

In this chapter, I explore:

- The history of global Anglicanism,
- The theological and cultural issues confronting our unity,
- The origins of the present crisis,
- My personal perspective rooted in culture and ministry, and
- My consolidated proposal for the future of Anglican unity under Archbishop Sarah's leadership.

This is not an academic treatise, though it draws upon theology and history. It is a pastoral reflection, written from lived experience, with the intention of provoking prayer, conversation, imagination, and hope. At its heart is one conviction:

> Unity is not the absence of disagreement. Unity is the triumph of love over disagreement, for the sake of Christ and his mission.

The story of Global Anglicanism: A family born in tension

Anglicanism was never designed to be a global communion. It emerged from the Reformation as a national Church, shaped by political compromise, theological breadth, and pastoral pragmatism. Yet these very features – its breadth, its adaptability, its commitment to Scripture and sacramental life – became the seeds of a worldwide family.

A Communion built on mission and migration

Anglicanism grew through a combination of missionary zeal, colonial expansion, trade, education, and migration. Missionary societies like the Church Missionary Society (CMS) and the Society for the Propagation of the Gospel (SPG) brought the gospel to Africa, Asia, Oceania, and the Caribbean. Yet while missionaries planted churches, it was indigenous Christians who gave Anglicanism its global character – translating Scripture, contextualising worship, and embodying the gospel in local cultures.

Theologically, this reflects the mystery of the Incarnation: *'The Word became flesh and dwelt among us'* (John 1:14). Anglicanism's global expansion mirrored this incarnational dynamic, as the gospel took on the particularities and textures of diverse cultures.

But the story is also marked by ambivalence. The gospel came alongside Empire, and the legacy of colonial power created painful imbalances that still shape relationships within the Communion today.

Provincial autonomy and the bonds of affection

The Anglican Communion is not held together by a pope or centralised curia. Each province is self-governing, yet united in shared history and relationship with Canterbury. This structure is profoundly theological: it reflects the early Church's pattern of local bishops united in shared faith rather than legal hierarchy.

Richard Hooker's vision of Scripture, reason, and tradition created a broad theological tent. This 'Anglican comprehensiveness' became both a strength and a weakness: strength because it allowed contextual adaptation; weakness because it made consensus difficult when new moral questions emerged.

The bonds of affection that hold the Communion together are relational, not juridical. They rely on trust, goodwill, and mutual respect – qualities that require constant renewal.

A communion of many voices

As Anglicanism took root in Africa, Asia, and Latin America, it developed new accents. African Anglicanism brought spiritual vitality and biblical intensity shaped by revival movements and persecution. Asian Anglicanism brought philosophical and contemplative depth; Caribbean Anglicanism brought liberative theology born from resistance and resilience.

The Communion's richness lies in this diversity. But diversity also creates tension when cultural frameworks produce different theological conclusions. The question becomes: *Can a global communion respect contextual theology while remaining recognisably one?*

The issues confronting global Anglican unity today

The Anglican Communion today stands at a convergence of profound forces – cultural, theological, political, historical, and spiritual. These forces do not simply press on the edges of unity; they challenge the very assumptions on which our unity has been built – for example, the long-held belief that shared liturgy and historic ties to Canterbury alone would be sufficient to maintain cohesion across radically different cultures and contexts, and the assumption that doctrinal disputes could be absorbed without structural reform because the 'bonds of affection' would always be strong enough to hold us together in times of strain. The issues we face cannot be separated neatly into 'doctrinal disagreements' or 'cultural differences.' They are intertwined, complex, and often emotionally charged, because they go to the heart of identity: Who are we as Anglicans? What holds us together? What do we owe each other?

In many ways, the contemporary struggles of global Anglicanism mirror the struggles of the early Church. The New Testament itself is a record of Christian communities wrestling with diversity, misunderstanding, and disagreement – from Corinth's factionalism to Galatia's legalism; from disputes about circumcision in Acts 15 to disagreements between Peter and Paul in Antioch. What kept those early believers together was not uniformity but shared fidelity to Christ, mutual submission, and a commitment to the Spirit's mission.

Today, several issues press upon us in similar ways.

For example, the disagreement over same-sex relationships mirrors the early Church's struggle with Gentile inclusion (Acts 15). Just as the apostles wrestled with how the gospel meets radically different cultures, so the Communion now wrestles with questions of human sexuality. Provinces in the Global North face pastoral realities shaped by safeguarding concerns, civil equality, and rapidly shifting cultural expectations. Meanwhile, many Global South churches minister in societies where same-sex relationships remain criminalised and deeply taboo. What appears to some as a question of justice appears to others as a question of holiness. Each side fears betraying the gospel, though in profoundly different ways.

Another example concerns diverging understandings of marriage and family. In many Western nations, marriage has been redefined both legally and culturally. But across much of Africa and Asia, marriage remains deeply embedded within extended family structures, communal honour, ancestral expectations, and kinship networks. These cultural differences inevitably shape how Anglicans understand Scripture on marriage, divorce, and fidelity, often leading to profound misunderstanding across provincial borders.

A third example is found in immigration, diaspora communities, and changing identity. The growth of diaspora congregations – from Nigerian Anglicans in London to Caribbean Anglicans in Toronto – has created both tensions and opportunities. These communities bring vibrant worship, strong biblical conviction, and different expectations of authority and pastoral leadership. Their presence challenges the inherited assumptions of historically English parishes, reshaping Anglican identity in ways that are both hopeful and, at times, disorienting.

Divergent biblical hermeneutics: Reading one scripture in many worlds

At the heart of Anglican contention lies Scripture – not its authority, but its interpretation. Few global traditions rely as heavily on Scripture as Anglicans do. Yet the ways in which we *read* Scripture differ profoundly, shaped by the worlds in which God has placed us.

In much of Africa, Asia, and the Caribbean, the Bible is read with a profound immediacy. Scripture speaks directly into contexts marked by poverty, persecution, corruption, spiritual warfare, fragile governance, and vibrant communal life. Texts of deliverance, holiness, obedience, judgement, and spiritual power resonate deeply. Miracles are not metaphor. The spiritual realm is not a symbol. The Bible is a living word that speaks with urgency.

In the West, where Christian imagination has been shaped by the Enlightenment, postmodernism, and the rise of humanistic ethics, Scripture is often approached with questions about context, history, anthropology, and psychology. The authority of Scripture is affirmed, but often understood through the lens of critical scholarship or pastoral sensitivity within secular settings.

These approaches are not mutually exclusive – indeed, both have deep roots in the Christian tradition – but they lead to dramatically different conclusions on questions of identity, sexuality, gender, justice, and moral reasoning.

The deeper theological question is not, 'Whose reading is correct?' but rather:

> Can a global Communion live with hermeneutical plurality without losing fidelity to the gospel?

This question, perhaps more than any other, defines our moment of crisis.

Human sexuality and marriage: The flashpoint of diverging moral imaginations

The conflict around sexuality is often framed as a disagreement about biblical morality. In truth, it is far more complex: it involves anthropology, trauma, cultural identity, intergenerational ethics, postcolonial tensions, and competing visions of pastoral care.

In many Western contexts, the Church ministers to LGBTQ+ individuals in societies where their legal, social, and relational equality is taken as normative. Pastoral care is framed around inclusion, safeguarding, and affirming identity. Sexuality is understood primarily through psychological and social lenses.

In much of Africa, sexuality is framed within communal life, traditional marriage structures, and biblical holiness codes. Many Anglican provinces operate in cultural environments where same-sex relationships are not only taboo but dangerous. Some face political pressure or risk violence. Others see the West's movement on sexuality as cultural imperialism dressed in progressive language.

These differences cannot be resolved simply through doctrinal debate. They touch the deepest questions of human identity:

- What does it mean to be created male and female?
- How do desire and holiness interact?
- How does Christian ethics relate to cultural norms?
- What is the role of the Church in shaping moral life?

The debate has become polarised, but its roots lie in the ways we form identity, understand community, and imagine God's holiness.

The question we face is not merely, 'What is the right answer?' but:

> How do we walk together faithfully when we disagree on questions that touch the human heart so intimately?

Colonial wounds and power dynamics: The ghosts that still walk among us

One cannot understand Anglican conflict without acknowledging the shadows of colonial history. Although many Western Anglicans do not consider themselves inheritors of colonial privilege, many Global South Anglicans still experience the Communion through the lens of historical power imbalances.

The Anglican Communion is one of the few Christian bodies whose structures still retain echoes of empire. Canterbury, once the centre of a colonial missionary network, still occupies symbolic primacy.

Decisions made in England or the USA reverberate throughout the world – sometimes welcomed, sometimes perceived as imposed.

For many African and Asian Anglicans, the fear is not merely theological disagreement but cultural erasure. They worry that global Anglicanism may become a vehicle for Western moral and cultural values – values they see as shaped by secularisation rather than Scripture. This fear is not irrational; it arises from centuries in which Western institutions controlled theological education, ordained leadership, and mission funding.

Conversely, many Western Anglicans now fear what they perceive as Global South attempts to assert doctrinal control over the Communion or reinterpret Anglican identity in ways that feel foreign to Western contexts.

The result is a relationship marked by mutual caution and misunderstanding.

Theologically, this raises a profound question:

> Can we practise mutual submission (Eph. 5:21) in a global fellowship where wounds of dominance and exclusion have not yet fully healed?

Until we answer that question honestly, unity will remain fragile.

The meaning of communion and the limits of diversity
The Anglican Communion is an ecclesiological experiment unlike any other:

- independent provinces,
- bound by history but not law,
- united by episcopacy but not centralised authority,
- diverse in theology yet committed to shared worship.

This structure allows extraordinary contextual flexibility, but it has never clearly defined how much diversity is too much. How far can contextual theology stretch before it becomes incompatible with shared communion? And who decides?

The debate on sexuality exposes this fault line. But beneath it lie deeper questions:

- What authority do the Instruments of Communion hold?
- Who speaks for the Anglican family?
- What binds us together: doctrine, liturgy, mission, or relationship?

Without clarity, every new disagreement becomes a threat to unity. We urgently need a theological – not procedural – vision of communion.

Economic inequalities: The unspoken power of money
Financial disparity shapes Communion dynamics in ways often left unspoken. The West funds theological colleges, mission agencies, clergy stipends, and development programmes across the Global South. This brings blessing – but also suspicion.

Is financial partnership an expression of Christian generosity – or a modern form of influence? Is refusal to follow Western theological developments perceived as risking funding? Do Global South provinces feel empowered to challenge partners who finance them?

The early Church shared resources so that 'none had need' (Acts 4:34), but without reproducing patterns of dominance. The Anglican Communion must learn to do the same.

Youth disengagement and secularisation: Two different worlds, one body
In Europe and North America, the Church faces

secularisation, institutional mistrust, ageing congregations, and the rise of the 'nones'. Survival is a daily question. Mission is often apologetic and defensive.

In Africa and parts of Asia, Anglicanism is young, vibrant, growing, and publicly influential. The challenge is not survival but formation – discipling young believers in contexts where prosperity preaching, political instability, and spiritual conflict abound.

Holding these radically different mission fields in one Communion requires a maturity and generosity we have not yet learned to practice fully.

The origins of the present crisis

Our present tensions did not emerge suddenly. They were woven gradually into the fabric of global Anglicanism through centuries of theological diversity, cultural movement, ecclesial evolution, and historical trauma. Understanding these origins is essential not to assign blame but to cultivate compassion.

A crisis long in the making: Diversity without a rulebook

From its birth, Anglicanism has embodied theological diversity. The Elizabethan Settlement intentionally created a Church broad enough to hold together Catholics and Puritans – an act of political necessity, theological innovation, and pastoral imagination.

This comprehensiveness continued into the global expansion:

- Evangelicals emphasised Scripture and personal conversion.
- Anglo-Catholics emphasised sacraments, mystery, and continuity with the historic Church.
- Liberals emphasised reason, conscience, and engagement with modernity.

- Charismatics emphasised spiritual gifts, revival, and the immediacy of the Holy Spirit.

These streams enriched Anglican life but also produced multiple identities within one Communion. The hope – beautiful but naïve – was that unity would hold simply because we desired it to. But desire alone cannot sustain a global fellowship without shared structures for discernment.

The Role of North American and English Developments

When the Episcopal Church in the USA consecrated Bishop Gene Robinson (an openly gay man) in 2003, it triggered a crisis already decades in the making. But the real shock was not the event itself – it was the realisation that provinces had no shared mechanism to discern or respond to such decisions.

This exposed:

- The lack of a common decision-making body
- The ambiguity of Canterbury's leadership
- The limits of Lambeth resolutions
- The fragility of 'bonds of affection'.

To some, the move represented prophetic justice; to others, theological betrayal. To some, it was pastoral compassion; to others, capitulation to secular culture.

The conflict became a symbol of broader anxieties about identity, authority, and truth.

The rise of alternative leadership structures: Parallel communions

As tensions deepened, provinces began forming alliances that bypassed traditional Anglican structures. The Global South Fellowship and GAFCON provided:

- theological clarity for conservatives,
- solidarity across continents,
- alternative forms of episcopal oversight, and
- a sense of missional purpose.

To some, these networks represent renewal; to others, schism. But their existence reveals a deeper truth:

> The Instruments of Communion have lost the moral authority to hold the family together.

Until this reality is faced honestly, unity will remain elusive.

A Personal Perspective: A Global, Cultural, and Relational Lens on Unity

My perspective on Anglican unity is shaped not only by theology and ministry but by biography, culture, survival, and a lifelong journey across two worlds. I stand in two Anglicanism – African and English – and I love them both. My calling has been shaped by the tension and beauty of living in this liminal space.

A childhood defined by conflict and survival: Theology from the cradle of suffering

My earliest theology was not learned in seminary but in crisis. Born during the Nigerian Civil War, in a hospital later bombed by the military, my life began in trauma. My mother carried me across 40 kilometres of danger to safety. Her endurance, faith, and courage were my first icons of God's love.

This experience shaped my theology profoundly:

- I learned that life is fragile.

- I learned that survival is grace.
- I learned that unity is not theoretical – it is a matter of life and death for communities torn apart.
- I learned that hope is not optimism but endurance.

Unity matters to me because division destroys. My childhood taught me that reconciliation is not optional – it is holy.

Ministry across cultures and continents: Two worlds, one calling

Serving in Nigeria and the UK has given me a vantage point few experience. I have preached under mango trees and beneath Gothic arches. I have led worship to the rhythm of African drums and to the sound of British choirs. I have prayed with farmers in rural English villages and with young families in London's multi-ethnic communities.

Each context revealed the gospel's beauty in different ways:

- Nigerian Anglicanism taught me fervent prayer, communal identity, spiritual warfare, and the power of Scripture.
- English Anglicanism taught me sacramental depth, pastoral patience, theological reflection, and liturgical beauty.

These worlds are different – but they are not mutually exclusive. My ministry has shown me that the Spirit of God is at work in all cultures, and that each culture reveals a facet of God's glory.

I have seen this truth in deeply practical ways. I remember leading worship in a Nigerian village where prayers were offered with a fervency that shook the dust beneath our feet. The women's guild sang with a joy that could lift the discouraged, and the men's fellowship prayed as though the walls between heaven and earth were tissue-thin. In that setting, faith was not an idea but a *lifeline*. Prayer was survival. Holiness was resistance. Scripture was the anchor of a people who knew suffering intimately.

Years later, I stood in a quiet English parish church, its ancient stone walls carrying the prayers of generations. There, elderly parishioners prayed with a gentle steadfastness that moved me just as deeply. Their faith was not loud – it was *faithful*. Their silence was not emptiness – it was *reverence*. Their careful reading of Scripture did not lack passion – it reflected decades of walking with God through grief, illness, austerity, and change. In their liturgy, I encountered a depth of sacramental beauty that taught me to slow down and listen for God in stillness.

I have also witnessed the Spirit's work in multicultural London, where a single Eucharist gathers worshippers from half-a-dozen nations. I have preached in congregations where a Ghanaian mother prays in tongues for her children's safety; where an elderly English widower offers intercessions shaped by a lifetime of service; where a young British-born Nigerian leads worship blending Hillsong with Igbo choruses; and where a Caribbean grandmother dances her offering down the aisle with quiet tears of gratitude. These gatherings taught me that identity is not a threat to unity – it is a gift to it.

In diocesan leadership, I have sat with clergy who worry about declining attendance in rural parishes, and with immigrant clergy who worry they will never be fully accepted in the structures of the Church. I have listened to white British parishioners grieving the loss of 'their' traditional church culture, and to African parents worried that their British-born children are drifting from the faith. All of them, in their own way, reveal something of the heart of God – a longing for belonging, a desire for meaning, and a hope for a future shaped by love.

And I have seen the Spirit move in unexpected places:

- in the boldness of a young curate leading prayer in the middle of a London market,
- in the calm of a Nigerian grandmother blessing her food-bank volunteer team,
- in the quiet courage of a British teenager taking confirmation vows despite her friends' mockery,
- in the dignified tears of an asylum seeker receiving communion after fleeing religious persecution.

These worlds are profoundly different. Yet in each, the Spirit whispers the same truth: *'You belong to one another.'*

This lived experience convinces me that unity is possible. Not because cultures are alike, but because Christ is present in all of them. Not because we erase difference, but because we honour it. Not because the path is easy, but because the Spirit leads us – again and again – into deeper communion.

A cultural lens of communion: Ubuntu and the body of Christ

Growing up in African communal culture, I learned *Ubuntu*: 'I am because we are.' Identity is shared. Conflict is handled through dialogue, elders' councils, storytelling, and reconciliation rituals. No one stands alone.

This worldview aligns deeply with Paul's vision of the Church as the body of Christ:

- many members,
- interdependent,
- suffering together,
- rejoicing together.

This is why I struggle when Anglican provinces walk away from one another at the first sign of disagreement. Family does not walk away. Family wrestles, forgives, listens, and journeys together.

A vocational calling to bridge-building: Standing in the gap

Throughout my ministry I have been drawn again and again into roles that require listening, translating, mediating, and bridge-building:

- between African and British cultures,
- between young and old,
- between evangelicals and catholics,
- between clergy and laity,
- between majority culture and marginalised voices,
- between global North and global South.

I have learned that unity requires:

- courage to speak truthfully,
- humility to listen deeply,
- compassion to understand pain,
- and patience to build trust.

My life experience has convinced me that unity is possible – not easy, not quick, but possible. And for this reason, I believe the Anglican Communion can be renewed.

Hopes for the future under Archbishop Sarah

A new season of leadership

Archbishop Sarah steps into her ministry at a pivotal moment. She has the capacity to rebuild trust, restore honest conversation, and model the humility and courage the Communion urgently requires. Her leadership carries the promise of a style marked not by power but by presence, not by authority imposed but by authority earned through listening, wisdom, and faithfulness.

My proposal for the future of Anglican unity

My proposal for the future of Anglican unity does not rest on structural reforms or doctrinal standardisation, but on a renewed commitment to the relational, theological, and spiritual heart of our Communion. The Anglican family – spread across continents, cultures, economies, and histories – cannot survive on administrative arrangements alone. What we need is a transformation of our imagination: a rediscovery of what it means to be one body in Christ (1 Cor. 12), held together not by uniformity but by love, humility, and mutual recognition.

The primary conviction that shapes my vision is this: **unity must be relational before it is organisational**. The Anglican Communion's genius is its interdependence – provinces free to govern themselves yet bound in mutual care. But interdependence cannot flourish without trust. And trust cannot flourish without honest listening. To renew unity, we must build spaces where provinces speak candidly, without fear of condemnation or suspicion, about the cultural, theological, and pastoral realities shaping their decisions. I have seen this dynamic in African village councils, in Igbo community gatherings, and in diverse parish meetings in London: healing begins when people feel seen, heard, and understood. This is a theological discipline – an echo of the incarnational God who listens before speaking, dwells before correcting, and embraces before instructing.

Secondly, unity requires a **decolonial humility** in how we lead and relate. As a priest formed both in Nigeria and England, I have lived within the tensions created by history. We cannot pretend that colonial legacies do not shape our present dynamics. Nor can we ignore the growing confidence and maturity of Global South Anglicanism. Unity will endure only if leadership – particularly from Canterbury – models the kenotic humility of Christ (Phil. 2:5–11), willingly laying aside assumptions of cultural centrality and embracing shared, global ownership of the Communion's identity and mission. This does not diminish the role of Canterbury; rather, it strengthens it by rooting it in service rather than authority, listening rather than instruction, fellowship rather than oversight.

Thirdly, unity requires that we **re-centre mission and discipleship** as our common ground. The early Church did not survive because it solved every doctrinal dispute; it survived because it preached Christ, formed disciples, shared resources, and lived the gospel in community. Where mission is shared, unity deepens. Where discipleship is vibrant, differences become less threatening. Our Communion must be inspired once again by a common missional imagination: proclaiming Christ in secularised societies, nurturing revival in the global South, engaging with youth across cultures, resisting injustice, and standing with persecuted Christians. When we look outward rather than inward, we discover one another anew.

Finally, unity requires a spiritual renewal grounded in **daily prayer, repentance, forgiveness, and mutual honour**. Structures cannot produce what only the Holy Spirit can give. I propose a season of intentional, Communion-wide prayer – a shared pilgrimage in which provinces repent of harms, forgive wounds, honour differences, and ask the Spirit to bind us together in love. My life story, beginning in the trauma of civil war and finding hope in God's mercy, has taught me this truth: healing is possible, reconciliation is real, and unity – though costly – is worth every sacrifice.

This is my proposal: not a programme, but a posture. Not a system, but a spirit. Not uniformity, but a renewed covenant of love grounded in Christ, empowered by the Spirit, and offered for the mission of God in our generation and the next.

Conclusion: Nothing Is Impossible With God

My life began in conflict yet has been shaped by grace. I believe in unity because I have lived its cost and its miracle. The Anglican Communion, with all its wounds and wonders, is still God's gift to the world. Through Archbishop Sarah's leadership, through our shared commitment, and through the renewing work of the Holy Spirit, deeper unity is possible.

The future of Anglicanism does not depend on winning arguments but on walking together in Christ.

And by God's grace – **nothing is impossible.**

PRAYER

Gracious and Eternal God, We lift before you your servant Sarah as she begins her ministry as Archbishop of Canterbury. Pour upon her an abundance of wisdom, courage, and compassion. Strengthen her to be a shepherd of unity in a Communion rich in diversity and longing for peace. Where there is division, grant her grace to speak peace; where there is hurt, grant her tenderness to heal; where there is confusion, grant her clarity of vision and courage of conviction.

Guide her to lead with humility and holy boldness, honouring every culture, nation, and voice within our global Anglican family. Surround her with wise counsel, steadfast friends, and the sustaining power of your Holy Spirit. Through her ministry, deepen the fellowship of the Communion and renew our hope in the possibilities of your kingdom.

Bless her, O Lord, and bless our Communion through her leadership. In Jesus' name. Amen.

10
In the Bleeding Silence

Mission and the Church of England

Chantal Noppen

Mission today, if it is anything at all, is a matter of listening for the silences, the breath held too long. For the stories cut short, spoken over or turned away. For the people who stopped speaking to the Church not because they stopped believing, but because they stopped being believed.

We live in a world tuned to noise, not nuance. Every day the volume rises, attention thins. And yet, amid the busy banter, there are people quietly bleeding. A Church that follows Jesus cannot afford to miss that.

In first aid training they teach you to slow down.
Pause.
Assess.
Check for danger.
Pay attention to the quietest ones.

Lowering ourselves, to kneel beside the wounded. Listen before you touch. Presence before instruction. Care before cure.

Every Archbishop, every minister, every Christian, every community, could do worse than start there.

If mission begins in the silences and wounds of real life, then Sarah Mullally's appointment feels profoundly hopeful. Her being embodies the listening, healing presence we sorely need. A nurse. A mother. A dyslexic in a word-heavy world. A woman navigating a still patriarchal institution. Someone who has spent years speaking into systems well-practised in tuning out.

So let us name the wisdom that the Church has often ignored; women's bodies. A rhythm of ebb and flow, of shedding and beginning again. An, at times, overwhelming rhythm that the institution has forgotten and does not value. Pain does not always signal failure; sometimes it signals possibility. If God became flesh in all its messy, bleeding reality, surely the Church can honour the embodied cycles that teach resilience, renewal and hope?

Instead, too often our truth is muted. Yet in that silence we bleed and in those cycles of dying and beginning, of hoping and losing, God is present. If the Church dared to trust the realities of women's bodies we might rediscover a more honest, humane, Christ-shaped presence in the world.

As a member of General Synod and co-author of the Clergy Babies Maternity Policy Audit, I have seen firsthand the fiercely competent, deeply human ministry of Archbishop Sarah. She carries humility with resolute dignity, in the face of attack, aware and accepting of her brokenness, yet hopeful for what God can draw from it. It's inspiring to be honest, but my goodness, I do not envy her.

I don't believe that Sarah has been elected because of her gender, to tick a box as a bargaining chip in the inclusive versus conservative tug-of-war. She is the right person because of who she is and how she is. And I believe we will be able to become a better Church because of this.

Yet I know that she is going to receive an alarming amount of abuse, threats and disrespect that will be exponentially increased because she happens to also be a woman. The complaints and criticisms will be disproportionate to anything her male predecessors received, and that simple truth needs to be said, and heard. Being a woman is not an unfortunate inconvenience we must simply 'stomach', but part of her God-given identity, one that widens the door for so many. Her appointment offers us a mirror, not to admire and preen, but to reflect, repent and reform. Living a leadership not about hierarchy but humility, not about status but service.

During the speech Bishop Sarah gave from Canterbury Cathedral, as part of the announcement to her election, she spoke of Jesus as our 'source and standard'. That phrase has stuck with me, rolling around in my mind and heart while I reflect on the profundity, simplicity and yet the power of it as a touchstone. Priests regularly ask what our ministry is meant to look like; how we are living into our calling. Framing Jesus not as an inert title, but a compass for determining our direction, invites a consciously radical honesty. That has the potential to utterly transform the mission of the Church in a living, dynamic, evolving and exciting way.

If the mission of the Church is formed by first passing through a lens of Jesus as 'source and standard' how might we be seen, understood and related to? How would it look to mirror Jesus, who listened and lingered, who sat down at tables he wasn't supposed to sit at, and asked questions no one else cared enough to ask. Who regularly broke protocol to meet the unspoken needs around him, prioritising people over policy. It would draw us closer to those who don't fit our boxes, whose lives filter experience differently, whose vulnerability exposes our fear and our rigidity. It would demand a humility and willingness to adapt and evolve our praxis when confronted with the sacred reality in our flawed humanity.

Most people find the halls of Westminster, bishops', and synod chambers utterly distant, irrelevant even immaterial. Yet at the heart of our Christian faith is the conviction that God is not remote but incarnate and intimately close. God who lived among us and still lives with us, through us, in us. God was, is and will always be, woven into the fabric of creation, whether or not that creation chooses to see, seek or encounter that truth.

Clergy often stand with a foot in both worlds, though most of those entrusted to our care have little awareness of the paradox. We can be found in the policy rooms, intertwined with the governance of the land and the gentle hum of institutional debate. But we also shelter in pub doorways, visit the sick and dying, feed the hungry, walk the streets, the estates, shops and playgrounds of the communities in which we live and serve. Those distant, abstract structures shape how we are enabled and guided to minister on the ground, yet though influential, they are disconnected from daily life. For all practical purposes, they are ignored as irrelevant.

This is why Sarah's appointment matters. Not because she is a woman holding the most senior post in the Church of England, with a pivotal role in the Anglican Communion, shattering the stained-glass ceiling, but because she is normal. Human. Formed not by ecclesial bubbles, a closed circle of specially chosen posh boys and predictable pathways, but from real life, shaped by work, family, and struggle. Her normal person-ness invites us all, clergy and lay, leaders and followers, whoever and however we are beyond our binary understandings, to reconsider our own calls.

Are we living in ways that embody Jesus as our source and standard?

That invitation and commission was given to us

all, diverse as we are, with no demands for conformity. For me, Sarah's appointment is profoundly hopeful, not for the title she will have, but for the possibility she embodies. For the silent value it raises amongst many of us who struggle to find our place or even dare to believe we should have a place of worth and value. For those of us who are so painfully aware of the ways we don't fit in, of how we disrupt the patterns that are preferred, her appointment offers us the chance to sing a new song into the silence where we haven't often felt invited or able to speak.

How might we have the courage, as a Church, to bring a medic's mindset to show that Christ is for everyone, whatever labels, identities or baggage they bring, and that the Church might, too, be for them. Led by care first and foremost, the reality and painful truth of life as lived, rather than cured or corrected to fit a conformist mould. Are we attending to the people, the rhythms, the silences of the world we are sent into, or are we only tuned in to the learned narrative we are told we must repeat and echo?

The world is not rejecting faith. The world is rejecting being dismissed. And if the Church can learn again to listen as Jesus listened, to love as Jesus loved, then perhaps we might still have something beautiful, truthful, and healing to offer. Which I believe the world is wordlessly crying out for. Silence can be a deafening expression of pain and of suffering, but bleeding does not always mean brokenness.

As the National Coordinator of Inclusive Church, coming from a background of ordained ministry in very economically deprived estates and communities, I see and hear the wounds and scars being carried by those around me. I share the frustration of feeling helpless to affect change and powerless to challenge the system. Yet somehow, within that, God ensures I am equipped for the journey. I live by a coal-stained beach, where the ebb and flow of the tide reminds me of the relative insignificance any one of us can have on the full scene. Here, cycles of deprivation and courage repeat like tides – building and breaking, hiding then revealing evidence of the painful heritage embodied here. Memories lingering long after the world that created them has gone.

Change is rarely without challenge and struggle, yet within the pain, there is also promise, hope and possibility, rising and releasing, dying and beginning again. In the forgotten, under-resourced, overlooked, deprived pit villages of my deanery, people do not receive the care they deserve. I take funerals for families still hurt and grieving their circumstances, circumstances thrust upon them by decades of neglect and hardship. So desperately in need of grace, hope and healing, yet not in regular connection with the church in their midst.

And yet their hearts are large, their willingness to help, protect and care for 'their own' is a beautiful thing. Sometimes intimidatingly scary in its intensity!

In this painful messy, often uncouth place, my middle-class self-absorption and assumptions are challenged. Here I am daily confronted with examples of how we can actually live out so much of what Jesus modelled, encouraged and championed.

There is often not the time offered, or taken, to understand the context and cause for what lies behind health challenges, declining mental health, anger or resentment. As a Church we too often fall into the trope of feeding people or fighting fires, without stopping to identify what's causing the hunger or fuelling the fire.

As any minority group will tell you, exclusion always harms. Impacting long past the occasion or experience of it. Change always hurts, it's hard, and it's scary. But Jesus didn't shy away from expecting or demanding change. He sparked a revolution in thinking and being. Such disruption is often a necessary first step in healing, and then in new growth. We must be willing to endure the pain of cleaning the wounds we have inflicted and endured.

Today, medical ethics are often summed up in the phrase 'First, do no harm' a contemporary rendering of the principle at the heart of the Hippocratic Oath. While the original never used those exact words, its intent was clear: to help and never injure. This guiding ethic remains foundational across medical professions and offers a striking lens for how the Church might frame its own mission.

We must move on from the habits of simply justifying the harm we cause as necessary for the addressing of sin, demanding repentance and correction. We must move beyond proscribing a specific way of being and conforming, as if that were the key to how we earn salvation and redemption to secure our place in the next life. As if a set of rules could simply be followed and the result guaranteed and achieved as the prize.

But as every medic, or anyone who has ever watched a medical drama knows, there are always exceptions. Nuances. Complications that make the reality more awkward. What may help someone, may harm another. We cannot apply rigid expectations and limitations on life, because life is complex, beautiful and variable.

Part of the mission of the Church is to reduce harm and increase hope. We must have the courage to tell the truth, to speak into the uncomfortable silence, to acknowledge and admit our failures and mistakes. Washing and binding the wounds, so we can forge a new path, walking faithfully alongside each other. Curating our lives so that they point to Jesus as source and standard.

Perhaps the real power of the invitation we have before us, with a nurse, a mother, preparing to step into the mantle of being Archbishop of Canterbury, is to reimagine our mission, our purpose, our praxis and direction as beginning with care, rather than correction? If mission shaped by compassion rather than conformity shaped our engagement, we could transform how we engage with the world, and it might just then transform us.

If the Church dared to trust the rhythms and realities of women's bodies, we might rediscover a more honest, humane, Christ-shaped presence in the world. Holiness is not threatened by a drop of blood, or by our existence being less than picture-perfect, we simply act like it is. If God can be found in cramps that do not wait for liturgical permission, then God can be found in every embodied ache of our communities, in the bleeding silence, in the powerlessness of being held ransom by our physical humanity. Because the Word became flesh, real flesh - not theological flesh, not metaphorical flesh - but sweating, aching, bleeding, laughing, body-that-smelled-by-the-end-of-the-day flesh.

Mission is far more intertwined with the physicality of living than we often articulate. Bodies that can be broken and fragile, attending and responding to nuances unknown. Not just absorbing noise, but taking in the myriad ways that God is with us, breathing into us, inspiring, challenging, changing with and healing through us. Our experiences of life, of living, of loving, of bleeding, of crying, of pain, sorrow and doubt, all these lay claim to the missional fingerprints we carry. Trying to detach our understanding of mission from our experience of living does a disservice to everyone.

Mission is being and bringing a sense of the Kingdom into the messy here and now. Spotlighting the transcendent presence and possibility of God, radical love and bottomless grace within the tangled mess of everyday life where waiting and bleeding are already part of the story. Not trying to isolate it and suggest it is 'set apart', untouchable and untarnished, but real, bruised, bleeding, healing.

Sarah's vocation has been shaped and nurtured by the tensions between aspiration and reality, body and expectation, institutional inertia and human hope. As a nurse, and a mother, she knows how to project calm assurance within chaos, how to share difficult truths, how to care when answers are incomplete or the full picture cannot be shared or explained. If mission is anything, it is just that, being present in the spaces where life is raw and painful. Where the bleeding silence echoes. It is noticing the person in the corner, the family struggling under the weight of expectation, the young person who stopped asking because they stopped being heard.

It is resisting the urge to tidy, to fix, to correct, before understanding. It is patience, humility, courage, and love, love that refuses to dismiss, that refuses to impose, that refuses to harm. Jesus as source and standard calls us to a mission that is radically alive, infuriatingly flexible, and profoundly relational. It is being unafraid to be found eating with outcasts, listening to the silenced, resting amid tumult, demanding justice for the ignored, praying into every shameful corner of doubt we try to hide. Weaving together and holding the fragile threads of the sacred and ordinary, broken and whole, mundane and the miraculous.

Sarah's leadership heralds a change that invites us to listen more deeply, to act more faithfully, to live more truthfully. To ensure our actions speak louder than our words. To not be distracted by hierarchy, by status, by the abstract rules of the institution, but attentive to the people in front of us, the rhythms of life and grief. Not louder, but braver.

In a world increasingly shaped by algorithms and artificial intelligence, authenticity matters more than ever. Mission cannot be automated; it is incarnational, relational, attentive. Noise is easy, nuance is holy, silence speaks. We are called to be a Church in and of a changing world, keeping pace with society, yet fused with truths that exist outside of time. Within the bones of our mission, must be embodied expressions that can speak of and into the heart of human experience, as well as pointing to hope-filled possibilities.

The one we follow modelled what it means to be a servant king, a healer who puts human soul-deep needs and identity above all else, and at the heart of divine action. When we do this, hope can take root, not in the abstract sometimes stagnant rules of the institution, but in the messy, beautiful realities of life.

This is the mission we are invited into, to listen deeply, love boldly and tread gently in a world that aches for grace, silently pleading for hope. To be a Church that first does no harm, speaks truth tenderly, holds space for the overlooked aspects of creation and resounds with the rhythm of real life lived. To be present and tuned in to where God is weaving through the world. To be open to finding answers in unexpected places and experiences of God far outside of the church building that boxes them in.

Words will not be what brings this into being. It is a connection of recognition that occurs at a deeper, wordless level. Presence over power. If Sarah can help us ask whether we are living in a 'first, do no harm' way, then her leadership will be a gift. Not because she will fix everything (she cannot), but because she may inspire us to notice the bleeding silences and respond with healing and hope rather than fear. Mission is sown and grown on common ground where respect, grace and space are shared. It belongs to all of us, the responsibility lies with all of us. The wellbeing of all must be prioritised, not just a privileged few. It is not on one person, one archbishop, to deliver and provide. The duty is mutual. We must all model the care we hope to receive. Taking time to pause, pray, assess, triaging situations we encounter and applying 'do no harm' as the doctrinal lens through which we can look, engage and reform our doing and being.

Only then might the Church heal herself and rebuild the trust we have broken. Only then might we have a right to expect to be respected, valued and turned to, as a source and standard for communities defined by love and care. I hope this is what we might turn towards under Sarah's leadership.

The future of mission will not be written in louder statements or tighter structures, but in the quiet courage of communities choosing presence over power, compassion over control. In this moment, the missional opportunity is wide open like never before, for the Church of England to reframe what it means to be a follower of Christ, to articulate in our actions what a Christian is. To show how we love, by how we live. That when we at last do come to our reckoning, we might hear a gentle whisper

> 'Girl, in your life you showed and shone
> Me. As your source and standard.
> In you, I am well pleased.'

This is the invitation before us now. And I am so here for it.

PRAYER

Holy and inspiring God,
You come close to those the world overlooks,
and hear those we often tune out.

We give thanks for Sarah,
called to lead with wisdom, with humility,
with courage.

Together may we have the patience
to honour life rhythms,
and courage to act with justice and love.

Bless the Church of England,
to embody your presence in every place,
to welcome all as they are,
and bear your Kingdom into the messy,
beautiful, painful, and joyful realities of this world.

Mould us into a people who first, do no harm,
speak truth with tenderness,
seek common ground,
and hold Jesus,
as source and our standard
before us always.

May your love reach every home and heart
where it has been forgotten, denied or withheld.
Amen.

Afterword

Rowan Williams, former Archbishop of Canterbury

The point of having any kind of ordained ministry in the Church is that there should be those whose primary task it is to help the Church be itself. This is true in a prison chaplaincy, a rural parish, a religious community, a diocese, or a – well, what, in the case of an Archbishop of Canterbury? Presumably in the context of the whole of a wider society in England. And – if now in an altered and even diminished way – the global Christian world as well. No minister of the gospel is there to make a name as a celebrity, a charismatic crowd-puller (that may or may not happen; if it does, there is, fortunately, plenty of resource to encourage scepticism and humility). But the real rationale is that they are there to keep telling the Church in whatever way is available what it actually is.

It is not a business or a 'movement' or a cult or an interest group. It is where God is acting to restore humanity in the divine image through the grace of Christ crucified and risen, so that the human world may see possibilities for transformation that would otherwise be in the realm of fantasy. Ministers of the gospel tell the story of *metanoia*, minds changed, horizons altered; of the imperative and the cost of seeing ourselves in a radically new way and turning to the light that shows this.

One of the gifts given to anyone with a loosely

defined wandering ministry – like bishops and archbishops – is the gift of witness. They are in a position to say to *this* local community, 'Let me show you what is to be learned from *that* local community – and let me carry to *them* the good news of what *you* are doing.' One bit of advice I'd want to give to any bishop or archbishop is simply to be ready to learn those stories and to pass them on and around. You're a switchboard (if you can remember back that far), a point through which communication – communion – passes.

If we don't have a lively and densely textured set of narratives like this, two things are likely to happen. We may be oppressed by other people's stories about us – by the Church that is 'narrated' by media and gossip. Or we may take refuge in abstract goals and strategies that connect very imperfectly to how people are actually encountering transformation.

Not in the least that this licenses us to gather round the campfire and exchange tribal chants that reinforce our sense of security and rightness. God forbid. If the job is to encourage people to be the Church, we need a sharp sense of what the Church isn't, and of where it is turning away from the chance to be itself. External challenge and critique ought to chime with or wake up our own sense of what's wrong – when we are consumed with anxiety about self-protection, looking good (or at least not too disastrously bad), limiting damage. It still feels to a very large number of people that our safeguarding culture is still dominated by these things, and not very visibly showing a readiness to repent and learn and keep asking what makes church unsafe for so many (ordained and lay) these days, a readiness to be called to judgment and renewal by the voices we prefer not to hear.

Being free from the compulsion to defend ourselves as Church only comes when we are confident enough of mercy to face the truth. A Church that is being itself is one that acknowledges without panic its failures, past and present, its inability to solve its problems and smooth out its conflicts. And this happens when we are first - and lastingly – absorbed in the reality of life in the Spirit: serious about worship, serious about the granular, embodied, local reality of God recreating lives in the divine image, serious about the desire to go on learning and having our hearts enlarged.

Second piece of advice, then? Be serious. No, obviously not humourless and earnest; but aware of the weight of the promise we are entrusted with, aware that it has the potential to astonish, terrify and release. An archbishop has some limited opportunities for this, but there will be quite a lot to stifle it – not least what I once called the default setting of thinking of the Archbishop of Canterbury as a rather enlarged version of faintly ridiculous clergy in sitcoms. You have to push back at this and you'll probably fail as your predecessors did, because there is something innately ridiculous about rather a lot of the theatre of ecclesiastical office; but by the grace of God there are moments – of loss, trauma, hard memory, and celebration too – where there is enough ambient seriousness to help you be and sound serious yourself. Recognize this, go with it. Philip Larkin's famous lines about how people are always surprising in themselves 'a hunger ... to be more serious' still reflect something truthful, and we shouldn't be afraid of it. When all's said and done, the Church is there to speak about death and what isn't contained by death, about hope when there is nothing obvious to hope for; that should be serious enough for anyone.

I notice that I've started writing as though I were directly addressing Sarah; and I suppose that's inevitable. I'm not praying that she – that you – will solve the problems, but that you will know where to feed your hope; that you will have breathing space in the middle of all the projections, positive and negative, to be where you can hear the good news of the Church's reality, so often in unexpected and marginal places – the odd joy of seeing the Spirit in the small and ageing congregation, in the special needs class, in the village agricultural project in a remote parish in Malawi, in a drop-in centre for the homeless in Sao Paolo … And yes, I am thinking back to what kept my faith alive as Archbishop, and wishing you gifts of the same order. All this happens because of God, not because of our strategies, essential as they are; all this happens whether 'the world', in the shape of online comment or whatever, notices or not.

If an archbishop has the freedom to listen and share good news, they will be doing what every ministry exists for, giving permission for the Church to be itself. And they will be anchoring all this, as a matter of routine, in the discipline of being there at table and pulpit in local churches whenever possible, to learn again what God is doing, and to repeat in context after context the central story of how God has done it and is doing it, the story of Christ opening wide his arms on the cross, bidding us welcome when our souls draw back.

There it is then: absorb and share the local stories; be serious. Make breathing space. Above all, keep saying to the Church, 'Don't forget, your "charter" is God's covenant, and that promise is not broken'. It is a promise to you as well as to the whole company of the faithful (and the not-yet faithful and the possibly-faithful and the plain bewildered).

Be sure of that, as you can be sure of all those people praying that you will help them be the individuals and the communities that God desires and nurtures. Your embassy is on behalf of the new creation – not a business or a 'movement' or a cult or an interest group, but the company that no one can number whose hope was and is in the Word made flesh.